# How to Pass
# AS Modern World History

**Martin Collier**

Heinemann

Heinemann Educational Publishers
Halley Court, Jordan Hill, Oxford, OX2 8EJ
a division of Reed Educational & Professional Publishing Ltd
Heinemann is a registered trademark of Reed Educational & Professional Publishing Ltd

OXFORD MELBOURNE AUCKLAND
JOHANNESBURG BLANTYRE GABORONE
IBADAN PORTSMOUTH NH (USA) CHICAGO

First published 2000

ISBN 0 435 32752 6

02 01 00
10 9 8 7 6 5 4 3 2 1

Designed and typeset by Wyvern 21 Ltd, Bristol

Printed and bound in Great Britain by The Bath Press Ltd, Bath

**Written sources acknowledgements**

The author and publishers gratefully acknowledge the following publications from which written sources in the book are drawn.

M. Clark, *Modern Italy 1871-1982* (Longman 1984): 84; M. Collier and P. Pedley, *Weimar and Nazi Germany 1919-1945* (Heinemann Educational Publishers 2000): 134A, 146D; D. Evans and J. Jenkins, *Years of Weimar and the Third Reich* (Hodder and Stoughton 1999): 117C; G. Katkov and H. Shukman, *Lenin's Path to Power* (McDonald 1971): 32B; C. Koonz, *Mothers in the Fatherland* (Jonathan Cape 1987): 145A; D. Moon, *The Russian Peasantry 1600-1930: The World the Peasants Made* (Longman 1999): 49A; A. Owings, *Frauern: German Women recall the Third Riech* (Penguin 1993): 145C; J. Vick, *Modern America* (University Tutorial Press 1985): 179D; J. Wheeler-Bennet (ed.), *Documents on International Affairs* (Oxford University Press 1934): 145B; J. Wheeler-Bennet, *Knaves, Fools and Heroes in Europe between the Wars* (Macmillan 974): 116B

The publishers have made every effort to trace the copyright holders, but if they have inadvertently overlooked any, they will be pleased to make the necessary arrangements at the first opportunity.

ii

# Contents

# Introduction

## What is AS Level?

AS Level History is intended to build on the skills and understanding gained at GCSE Level. Studying AS Level History will prepare you for further study and a range of career opportunities. It will give you a more sophisticated understanding of history whilst helping to develop your evaluation and analytical skills. AS Level History can be taken in combination with virtually all other subjects on offer to you. The skills and perspective it gives you are recognised by education institutions and employers.

The new AS examination takes a modular approach. This means that you will study your AS in three units. Many units will have an examination in January and June.

## How to use this book

This book will help you to succeed in your **AS Level History examination**. The opening chapters offer essential advice on how to answer the main types of questions set by the various Awarding Bodies (OCR, AQA and Edexcel).

The book contains three main sections:
- **History skills**. In this section there are questions in the different styles of the three examination boards. You should practise writing answers to the questions in this section. Tackle questions in the style of the Board you are registered with. It is good practice to try to write answers in the time allocated to each question.
- **Historical topics**. This content section gives a summary of the main events of each period you are studying. You could use this summary to refresh your memory before trying to answer related questions, or to help with your revision. This section of the book also looks at the different ways in which the Awarding Bodies ask questions.
- **Assessment sections**. At the end of each chapter there is an assessment section. In this section you are given examples of examination questions and guidance on how to answer those questions. Further questions are included at the end of most chapters for you to practice your answering skills.

# Chapter 1
# Answering essay questions and structured questions

The aim of this chapter is to introduce you to some of the important skills you will need to acquire to succeed at AS Level History. You should refer back to this chapter when completing some of the assessment tasks later in the book. This will help you to direct certain skills at relevant questions.

## Essay questions

An essay question is a single question. It asks the candidates to argue a response to a particular question. Essay questions vary in style and scope. However they demand a *direct* response. Here are examples of course essay questions from AQA:

a  Why did the communists win the Civil War in Russia 1918–21?

b  For what reasons were the governments of the Weimar Republic unable to prevent political collapse during 1930–32?

## Structured questions

These questions are broken into more than one question known as sub-questions. However, although there is more than one part to a structured question, there is usually only one theme. Here is an example of a structured question from Edexcel Unit 2:

a  Describe how Lenin's economic policies in the period up to 1924, tried to solve the problems facing the Bolsheviks in 1918.

b  Explain why these policies aroused opposition within the Bolshevik Party and within the USSR.

As you can see, the sub-questions ask the candidates to 'describe' and 'explain' which are different skills. However the theme of Bolshevik economic policy 1918–24 is shared.

## Questions that require an analytical response

The ability to analyse is one of the most important skills that you need to develop when studying AS History. Analytical questions ask you to explain why or how, rather than to describe. Here are four examples:

1  Why did Germany suffer from hyperinflation in 1923?

2  Why did Lenin's economic policies in the period 1919–24 arouse opposition within the Party and the Soviet Union?

**3** Do you agree with the view that the main cause of the Great Depression in the United States of America in the 1930s was overproduction in the 1920s? Explain your answer fully.

**4** Compare the importance of any three factors which explain why the First World War broke out.

You can spot an analytical question by asking yourself the following: 'Am I required to present an argument and interpretation in response to this question?'

## A line of argument

In all your answers you need to develop an argument which directly addresses the question. Your line of argument will lead you to make a judgement in response to the question. This is important if you are to achieve top marks for your answers. Your line of argument will be valid if it is backed up with evidence. Remember that many different lines of argument can be taken.

## Prioritising

When analysing a particular issue, you will have to weigh up a variety of factors. As part of your line of argument, you should try to prioritise the factors. This means choosing one factor as the most important in relation to the others. You will then need to explain why this particular factor is the most important and why other factors are less so.

## Using evidence

Any line of argument must be backed up with evidence which is accurate and detailed. The information you use will make your argument a valid one. Analysis does not work without evidence to back it up.

## Complexity

Your line of argument must be complex if it is to show a good understanding of the real-life events that occurred. You will be able to show that the issue you are analysing is complex. The way to do this is to complete a plan which includes more than one line of argument or develops the one line of argument fully.

## Interrelation of factors

You should explain in detail how various factors are related to each other. For example, you should make it clear that you have an overview of the relationship between the different causes; how one factor leads to another; how one factor makes another more significant; how some of the short-term causes relate to the long-term causes.

## Historical interpretations

Where relevant, you might explain how and why historians differ in their accounts and explanations of what happened. However you should not simply describe different interpretations. Your own interpretation is the most important.

## How to analyse

The next stage is to understand how you analyse. The following pages contain some points of advice.

## Planning

The most important step when writing a response to an answer is to make a plan. **You should never start answering a question without making a plan first**. If you are answering a question for homework, you should spend a fair amount of time on your plan. Once you have worked out a clear plan, you have almost answered the question.

A word of warning, however. In an examination, when time is at a premium, you are advised not to spend too much time on your plan. For example, if you have 30 minutes' writing time, you should spend no more than 3 minutes planning.

Your plan should include the following:
* the lines of argument you intend to use
* a structure for your ideas
* a list of what you are going to put in each paragraph.

There are essentially two types of analytical questions.
a  *Why?* This type of question asks you to analyse the causes or consequences of an event or phenomenon. To answer a 'why?' question you must follow these steps in your plan:
   * identify the different factors central to the question
   * develop a line of argument by prioritising your factors.
b  *To what extent?* This type of question demands that you explain the extent of the impact of a person, or event, phenomenon, idea etc. The answer to this question is invariably 'up to a point...but' or 'to a certain/considerable/minimal extent...but'. In your plan, therefore, you should include points which show the extent, eg impact, and the 'but/however' point.

Example of a *Why?* question. Here are some guidelines for writing a plan in response to one of the example questions given above and here. (It is a question in the style of those set by Edexcel.)

Q  **Why did Lenin's economic policies in the period 1919–24 arouse opposition within the Party and the Soviet Union?**

*Lines of argument*

1  Opposition to Lenin's policies from within was primarily ideological. It came from those who opposed Communism and those who felt the Revolution had been betrayed.
2  Opposition was aroused in different groups who suffered the consequences of the economic policies.
3  Opposition can be seen in the context of the wide-ranging debate about the future of Soviet society.

*Structure*

- **Introduction** The success of your response rests on being able to answer the question directly from the start. Therefore, you should use your lines of argument to write the introduction.
- **Paragraph 1** Explain the ideological opposition of the Whites etc. to War Communism and of those within the ranks of the Bolsheviks to NEP.
- **Paragraph 2** Explain the opposition to War Communism due to the grievances of peasant workers who suffered shortages. Mention the protests of February 1921 and Kronstadt, 1921. There was opposition and resentment towards NEP men.
- **Paragraph 3** Explain opposition to economic policies because of the intensity of debate about the economic future of the Soviet Union.
- **Conclusion**. Here you briefly reinforce your argument. The conclusion is a useful place to make a sustained judgement.

Example of a *To what extent?* question. Here are some guidelines for writing a plan in response to a questions in the style of those set by OCR.

Q  **To what extent did Stalin bring about change in the Soviet Union in the 1930s?**

*Lines of argument*

1  Stalin changed the Soviet Union to a considerable extent.
2  The Soviet Union was changed most significantly in the economic sphere through collectivisation and industrialisation.
3  However the extent of change should be qualified. Many changes were greater than they seemed because of propaganda.

*Structure*

- **Introduction** Use the lines of argument above in your introduction.
- **Paragraph 1** Argue that the most considerable change was in the economic sphere.

6

- **Paragraph 2** As part of the economic change there was a social revolution in education and through the purges.
- **Paragraph 3** Purging also brought a political change.
- **Paragraph 4** For some groups in society change was not great, eg women. Propaganda also exaggerated some of the change.
- **Conclusion**. Briefly you should reinforce your argument.

## How to sustain an argument

The next part will cover some useful tips to help you sustain an argument.

1 In your answer, use words taken from the question. So, if the question is about 'stability' in Weimar Germany then use the word 'stability' in your answer.

2 At the start of each paragraph it is important that you use words and phrases which lead into analysis. Phrases to use include:
- It can be argued that . . .
- it is clear that . . .
- the most important point to consider is . . .
- without doubt, the most significant reasons for . . . is . . .
- essentially, . . .

3 When writing analytical answers you should avoid starting a paragraph with phrases or statements which will lead you into a narrative answer. Try to avoid constructions like:
- in (followed by a date) . . .
- the following year . . .

## Description questions

You will come across questions in some of the specifications which ask you to *describe*. Describing is one of the more difficult skills you will have to use. Sometimes questions which ask you to describe will start with the word 'describe'. However, you might be asked to describe without the word 'describe' being in the question. Here is an example:
- What was Trotsky's role in the Bolshevik victory in the Civil War 1918–21? You can spot a 'describe question by asking yourself the following question: 'Am I being asked to give an account of the main features/events/personalities?'

If you are then you will need to give a description. For the above example you are expected to write a detailed description of Trotsky's role and his contribution to victory.

Here are two further examples of this type of question:

Q 1 **In what ways was Germany able to maintain any kind of stability in the period 1923–29?**

Q 2 **Describe the weaknesses of the Italian Liberal State 1918–22.**

These questions are *not* asking you to explain why things happened. Instead, they are asking you to select relevant material which will help you to describe in detail the main feature(s) of the question.

## Planning

You should still plan your answers to these questions before you start writing. Instead of placing your key arguments at the start of the answer, you should outline your **key themes**. Otherwise, you should follow the structure for a plan as explained above.

Here some key themes that you might wish to use in response to one of the example questions mentioned above.

**Q    Describe the weaknesses of the Italian Liberal State 1918–22.**

- The Liberal State was weakened by the introduction of mass politics and the emergence of mass Catholic and Socialist parties.
- The First World War, Versailles, and economic and social unrest created the conditions in which the Liberal State was plunged into crisis.

## Style

You need to show that you have very clear understanding of the significance of events and be able to link them back to the question. Below is an extract from an answer to the question we are considering. The candidate is attempting to show how the Fiume episode was important in determining the weaknesses of the regime.

The disappointment amongst nationalists at the Versailles Treaty (which they called a 'mutilated victory') was to weaken the Liberal State further. When Nitti's government failed to press Italian nationalist claims over Fiume at Versailles, the nationalist Gabriele D'Annunzio acted independently. In September 1919, D'Annunzio marched into Fiume with 2000 supporters, and declared the town annexed to Italy. This was done with the knowledge of the Italian Army. Not only were his actions extremely popular, they legitimised extra-parliamentary action and, for 15 months, stood as a symbol of the weaknesses of parliamentary government.

## Answering questions set by Edexcel (Units 2 and 3)

In these units you will have to answer questions that demand an analytical answer and questions that require detailed description and explanation in the answers.

## Analytical answers

Here are two examples of questions requiring an analytical answer:

Q 1 **Why did Martin Luther King promote peaceful methods of campaigning for Civil Rights?**

Q 2 **Why did Germany experience political instability in the period 1918–23?**

In answering these questions you need to do the following:
- sustain an argument throughout your answer
- support your argument with selected information
- prioritise the relative importance of the factors
- organise your answer into paragraphs.

## Answers with detailed description and explanation

Here are two examples of questions demanding this type of answer:

Q 1 **Describe the role played by Martin Luther King in the struggle for Civil Rights in the 1960s.**

Q 2 **In what ways did Germany regain diplomatic respectability in the period 1924–29?**

In this type of question you need to:
- write a detailed explanation in response to the question
- use well-selected evidence – the material you use must be directly relevant to the question, and accurate
- cover the relevant areas as demanded by the question
- organise your work into clear paragraphs.

## Answering questions set by AQA

AQA also set two types of question: essay questions without sources and structured questions.

## Essay questions without sources

Here are two questions of this type which demand an analytical response.

Q 1 **How successful was the 1905 Revolution in achieving political reform in the period up to the outbreak of the First World War?**

Q 2 **How successful was Stalin in removing opposition in the Soviet Union in the 1930s?**

To answer this type of question you must:
- make a judgement which responds directly to the question and is explicit
- show an understanding of the question by using appropriate evidence to back up a balanced and well-structured explanation.

## Structured questions

You will be asked analytical questions with different marks allocated to each part. Here is an example:

**Q a)** Explain why Truman developed the policy which was later known as the Truman Doctrine. **(7)**

**b)** How successfully did the United States contain communism in the period 1947–53? **(15)**

There are some important points that you need to be aware of when dealing with these questions.

• The skills needed are the same as for other questions: you need to plan and argue well throughout your answer.

• Pay attention to the marks awarded for each part of the question. In your plan for the 7-mark question you might only have two points of argument, whereas in your plan for the 15-mark question you might have three points of argument.

• Allocate your time according to the marks. You have less time to write the 7-mark part. Therefore, your paragraphs should be a little shorter.

For both types of question covered above it is essential that you follow these guidelines.

• **Analyse.** As has been suggested above, you must analyse throughout your response to the question.

• **Evidence.** Your line of argument must be backed up with accurate information.

• **Balance.** Cover all the parts of the question in a balanced way.

• **Attempt to offer judgement.** This might be in the conclusion, but you should try and make judgements throughout your answer.

• **Structure.** You must try and structure your responses into paragraphs. You will be marked on the quality of your written English.

## Coursework

Two of the three Awarding Bodies, AQA and Edexcel, give you the opportunity to complete one of your AS modules via coursework. Below is advice on how to undertake coursework in each case.

**AQA, Course essay.** For Module 3 you will be asked to complete a course essay. The main focus of the questions of the course essay is on explanation. Below are examples of the types of questions you might be asked:

Explain why...?

With what success...?

Examine the factors..?

It is most important to try to prioritise the factors in order of importance, and to draw conclusions in relation to the question. The course essay title will be sent to your school/college two weeks before you are to write your response under timed conditions. This will give you two weeks to prepare for the writing of the essay. You will be allowed to use notes when writing your essay so you must try and plan the essay thoroughly in advance. However, your notes must not include a fully written out answer to the question.

**Edexcel, coursework.** As an alternative to the written examination for Unit 3 you may well be entered for the coursework assignment Unit 3c. The content of the coursework assignment is at the discretion of your teachers. However the unit of work you will study will be based on the significance of key individuals and/or events in depth.

You coursework assignments will be divided into two parts:

Part A is based on a response to sources. You will be asked to interpret and evaluate sources in the same kind of way as in Unit 1. There will be 10 marks awarded for this question and a word limit of 500 words. Here are examples of the style of questions asked in Part A.
- How far does the evidence of the sources provided suggest that the First World war was caused by Germany?
- How far do these sources support the statement that 'the root cause of the First World War was instability in the Balkans'?

Part B will consist of a question which will focus on the causes/consequences of a major event or development. There will be 50 marks awarded for this question and a word limit of 1700 words. You will be expected to do the following:
- write in an analytical fashion in response to the question (see Chapter 1 page 4)
- show an understanding of the relationship between causes/consequences
- where relevant you should refer to the appropriate views of historians.

Here are some examples of the style of questioning in Part B of the coursework.
- Why did the North Vietnamese win the Vietnam War?
- What were the consequences for Spain of Franco's victory in the Spanish Civil War?

Before you start writing your coursework, here are a few tips:
- do not leave your coursework assignment to the last minute
- use your teacher for advice
- plan your coursework thoroughly before you start writing
- make sure that your written style is concise and to the point
- do not exceed the word limit of the coursework
- check your coursework thoroughly before you hand it in
- your teacher might have a preference for how the coursework is written

up, either by hand or typed. If you have access to a computer there are benefits to typing your work up; in particular the work is easy to read and you can make corrections more easily.

## Answering questions set by OCR (Unit 3)

Here is an example of the type of question which will be set in this unit. The first part of the question will ask for explanation, the second part for analysis.

**Q a) Identify and explain the reasons why Mussolini fell from power in 1943.** **(30)**

## Explanation

There are some general points to consider when answering questions like this.

- Choose factors that you feel you can explain well and that are suitable for explanation. Here are some examples of factors you might use: food shortages and rationing, economic failure, military defeat, disillusionment amongst the establishment.
- You must explain the key issues in the question. In the example above the key issues are the reasons for Mussolini's downfall.
- Your answer must focus on explanations. You must not simply tell the story of his downfall.
- You must use historical knowledge which is accurate and you must communicate it well.
- Your answer must be well organised. The key to this is planning. When you write your answer it should be structured into clear paragraphs. There must be an introduction and a clear conclusion.

Here is an example of how you might answer this question.

> The Monarchy maintained its power and influence despite the fact that Victor Emmanuel seemed to accept fascist policy without question, himself signing decrees ranging from the anti-Semitic legislation of 1938 to the abolition of the Chamber of Deputies a year later. Despite this apparent subservience, and that the Monarchy lost its powers of selection over ministers and even the royal succession to the Grand Council in November 1928, it should be pointed out that it was the King who sacked Mussolini in 1943. As the Monarchy, in consultation with the establishment, brought Mussolini into power, so it removed him. Therefore, it should be argued that the disillusionment of the establishment as represented by the King was fundamental in explaining the fall of Mussolini.

**Q b) Assess Mussolini's success by 1939 in making Italy prosperous and politically stable.** **(60)**

### Assessment

There are some general points to consider when answering questions which ask you to assess.

- Identify the key issues first of all. In this case they are 'prosperous' and 'politically stable'.
- You should show an understanding of the *extent* of, in this case, success. The answer to the question will often be 'up to a point...but'.
- You must deal with both aspects of the question.

# Chapter 2
## Answering source-based questions

The source-based questions for all specifications are very similar. We will look at the different types of questions that you will find, and how you can go about tackling these. Many source-based questions ask you to evaluate the sources. However, it should be noted that on occasions a source is used only as a stimulus.

### Comprehension questions

Many source-based exercises start with a comprehension question. Often only a few marks are awarded to the question. Here are examples of comprehension questions.

Q 1 **Using Source C and your own knowledge, explain what these statistics tell us about Russian economic expansion in the period 1900–14.**

Q 2 **Study Sources A and B. What can you learn from these sources about the boom in the US economy in the 1920s?**

Q 3 **Study Source B. Explain the significance of the statements in this source in the context of Stalin's rise to power.**

To answer this type of question you should:
- ask yourself what is the main point of the source
- read between the lines of the source to work out its real message or meaning
- show that you understand the issue(s) relating to the source
- **never** simply write out what the source says in your own words.

### Questions that ask you to make a value judgement

Many questions ask you to make a decision about the value of a source. Here are some examples.

Q 1 **Study Sources 1 and 2. Assess the value of these Sources to an historian studying the reasons why support for the Nazis grew in the 1920s and 1930s.**

Q 2 **Study Sources 3 and 4. Assess the value of these Sources to an historian studying Lenin's role in the October Revolution in 1917.**

If you are asked about the value of a source, you need to ask yourself the following questions. However, not all the bullet points will be appropriate to the type of source or question asked.

How to Pass AS Modern World History

- Who was the author of the source?
- What was his or her purpose in producing the source?
- Was the source produced as propaganda?
- Has the author deliberately distorted the evidence?
- What was the situation of the author?
- Was the author in a position to know about the subject of the source?
- In your view, has the author used the full range of sources available at the time?
- Has the author dealt with the different views from the time?
- How has the author dealt with gaps in his or her evidence: are they acknowledged or simply ignored?
- Does the interpretation reflect the kind of attitudes held at the time of writing?

It should be noted that the value of a source can be partly assessed by matching it to what you know.

## Questions about utility

You might be asked how useful a source is. Here are some examples of questions which ask you to judge the utility of the sources.

**Q 1 Study Source A. How useful is this source as evidence of Stalin's intentions in 1929?**

**Q 2 Study Sources 3 and 4. How useful are these two sources as evidence about the impact of the Wall Street Crash?**

To produce a top-quality answer about utility, you must:
- discuss both the positive value and the limitations of the source(s), pointing out any gaps in the evidence
- compare positive points, limitations and reliability of the sources when more than one source is offered
- compare the usefulness of the source(s) when viewed in the light of your own knowledge
- mention the extent to which the author's views were typical of the period.

Bear in mind that the usefulness of a source depends on the questions asked of it. For example, you might consider whether a particular source can be corroborated (backed up) with other evidence. It is important to realise that sources can be useful even if they are not reliable.

## Questions about the reliability of a source

You might be asked about the reliability of a source or a selection of sources. In any answer on reliability, you must make sure that you include your own knowledge to back up the points you have made. The situation and purpose of the author is the key to working out the reliability of a source. Here are two examples of this type of question.

**Q 1** **Source F is statistical information, Source G is an extract from an interview. Which of the two sources is more reliable for an historian studying inflation in Germany in 1923?**

**Q 2** **How reliable is Source 3 for an historian studying the causes of the Wall Street Crash?**

To answer these and similar questions, you are expected to address the following points:
- was the author of the source in a position to have accurate information?
- what was the purpose and the motive of the author in producing the source?
- who was the intended audience for the source and does this effect the source's reliability?
- are there examples in the source of (either deliberate or unconscious) bias?
- you have to ask 'reliable as evidence of what?'

## Questions about different interpretations

Here are two examples of this type of question.

**Q 1** **Source C is a letter, Source D is a cartoon. Why are these two interpretations of the end of the Battle of Stalingrad so different?**

**Q 2** **Study Sources B and C. Compare and explain the different interpretations of the causes of the Night of the Long Knives.**

When trying to determine why interpretations differ, you should think about these questions.
- What was the situation of each author?
- Under what conditions were the sources produced?
- What was the political background?
- What were the events surrounding the writing of the source?
- Could these have influenced its contents?
- When were the sources written?
- What was the purpose of each author?
- Why did the authors produce the sources?
- Who was the intended audience of each source?
- What is the nature of the sources (e.g. newspaper or cartoon – this will influence what the source says)?
- Is there any political bias?
- Is the source an example of propaganda?

## Comparison of sources

This type of question is set by OCR and Edexcel. Here is an example of a question which falls into this category.

**Q  Study sources A and B. Compare Stalin's intentions and aims in 1931 according to Sources A and B and explain the differences.**

To achieve a top mark you must:
- discuss the agreements/similarities between the sources, as well as the disagreements/differences
- compare the sources for authenticity (whether they are authentic or fabricated)
- compare the nature of the sources
- compare the completeness of the sources and ask how typical they are
- use your own knowledge to answer the question.

## Questions which ask you to draw conclusions

This type of question asks you to make conclusions about the past from the particular sources (and their interpretations), in the light of an evaluation of the evidence. Often this type of question is posed as the last question of a sources exercise. You are asked to use some of the sources and your own knowledge. Below are some examples of this type of question. All the boards start their questions by asking you to study the sources and to address the question by using your own knowledge. But they ask their questions in different ways:

**Q  1  (In the style of AQA)**
**How was the German government weakened as a result of the challenges it faced in the period 1918–23?**
**Q  2  (In the style of Edexcel)**
**Do you agree that the Wall Street Crash was caused by overproduction?**

To answer these questions you should:
- sustain an argument and draw conclusions using the sources and, importantly, your own knowledge
- interpret the meaning of the source(s) in the light of the question
- show that you understand the question by making a clear judgement, perhaps in the conclusion
- prioritise the factors which you are discussing.

The evaluation and interpretation of each source, and the application of your knowledge, does not have to be lengthy. You must refer to the source, however, and you must use you own knowledge to inform your judgement.

OCR questions are slightly different. Here is an example:

**Q  Using all the sources and your own knowledge, explain the priorities of Nazi economic policy in the period 1933–39.**

This style of question demands the same skills as listed above in relation to AQA and Edxecel questions, but also a little more. You also need to:

- evaluate the sources, again drawing on your own knowledge
- make a judgement about their utility and reliability, given what they say and how this compares to what you know
- make a judgement about the author, and his or her situation and motives against what you know.

Here is an example of how you might answer this question. Note that the candidate interprets the source, uses her own knowledge and evaluates the source as evidence.

> After coming to power the most important economic priority for the Nazi leadership was the reduction in unemployment which stood at about a third of the workforce in 1932–33. That this was important to the new regime can be seen in Hitler's claim in Source D that the government's priority was to save the German worker by a massive attack on unemployment. Indeed German State investment increased by 6.4 billion RM between 1933–36. However Source D has its limitations. Hitler's 'Appeal to the Nation' speech was very much aimed at calming fears of Nazi radicalism at home and abroad. Therefore, it does not mention rearmament which was the other main priority even in 1933 and on which much of the extra 6.4 billion RM mentioned above was spent.

## Extended source-based questions

AQA sets this type of question which requires an extended answer in response to a source-based question. Here are two examples:

**Q  1  Study sources A and B and use your own knowledge.**
   **Why was complete control over their people so important to Mussolini and Hitler as dictators?**

**Q  2  Study Sources A and B.**
   **How did the Tsarist regime survive the 1905 Revolution and attempt to strengthen its position afterwards?**

To answer this type of question you must:

- make a judgement which directly responds to the question and is explicit
- show an understanding of the demands of the question by selecting material from the sources and your own knowledge.

# Chapter 3
# Russia and the Soviet Union, 1900–49

## Section 1: Russia c. 1900–16

### Industrial growth

Despite years of depression in the early years of the twentieth century, the Russian industrial economy boomed again in the years running up to the First World War.

- Between 1907–14, industry grew at an average of 6.25% per annum.
- Industry was concentrated in large enterprises. By 1914 over 40% of the industrial workforce worked in 344 plants, each with over 1000 workers.
- During this period, the state invested in the railways, although the level of investment was low in comparison to the 1890s. Between 1907–13 around 1000 km of track was laid each year. Total mileage was around 76,000 km in 1914.
- Demand was created by new contracts to supply the Russian Navy with warships.
- Improved prices for agricultural produce after 1906 helped to create some domestic demand for consumer goods and domestic investment overall in this period outstripped that from abroad – 913 million roubles as opposed to 284 million between 1909–11.

### Results of economic change

Economic change brought with it social tension, unrest and demands for political reform.

- The industrial workforce was not a large proportion of the Russian population, numbering only 1.7 million (1.28%) in 1900 and still only 2.3 million (1.4%) in 1913. However, concentration of the industrial workers in cities, and their poor working conditions and pay, made them a potential threat to social stability.
- In 1895, the **Union for the Struggle for the Liberation of the Working Class** was set up to support striking workers, such as the 30,000 St Petersburg cotton spinners who were involved in a bitter dispute with their employers in 1896–7.
- These strikes were countered by further repressive measures, including the creation of a factory police force in 1899.
- In 1898 the **Russian Social Democratic Workers' Party** was set up.

## Further unrest 1901–05

- An economic downturn at the turn of the twentieth century led to a wave of strikes throughout the country, such as that at Rostov in 1902.
- Despite the attempts between 1901–05 of various supporters of the autocracy, e.g. Sergei Zubatov and Father Gapon, to set up unions or workers' societies not influenced by socialism, the attitude of the State to the proletariat continued to be hostile.
- The burden of exploitation fell equally on the peasantry and 1902 saw insurrections in the Ukrainian districts of Poltava and Kharkov. Such unrest was not inspired by Marxist thought, but it spurred the development of a political movement based on such ideology.
- In 1902 Lenin published **What is to be Done** which formed the basis of revolutionary Leninism.
- The following year the Russian Social Democratic Workers' Party divided into two factions: the **Bolsheviks** led by Lenin and the **Mensheviks** led by Martov.
- Pressure for democratic reform was centred around the **Union of Liberation**, created in 1904 by Milyukov and Struve, and which was radical in its demands for social justice.

## The Russo-Japanese war, 1904–05

The Russo–Japanese War proved to be the catalyst for the Russian Revolution in 1905.

- Russian expansionism in the Far East resulted in conflict with Japan and humiliating defeat at **Port Arthur** in December 1904.
- At sea, the Russian fleet was destroyed at the battle of the **Tsushima Straits** in May 1905.
- Each defeat provoked demonstrations which were also partly fuelled by continuing industrial unrest.
- By the **Treaty of Portsmouth**, signed in September 1905, the Russians recognised Japanese influence in Korea and were forced to end Russian imperial hopes in the east.

## The 1905 Revolution

- In January 1905 there was a strike at the Putilov metal works in St Petersburg.
- On 9 January 1905, **Father Gapon** led a march of the strikers to the Winter Palace with the intention of petitioning the Tsar. Father Gapon was the organiser of a government-sponsored union, the **Assembly of Factory Workers**.
- The crowd was attacked by police and Cossacks. There were many casualties on what was to become known as **Bloody Sunday**.
- Order was temporarily restored to St Petersburg but industrial unrest

spread. It was organised by newly-formed **soviets** (elected councils of workers).

- The first soviet was formed in the Urals in April. By far the most important soviet was in St Petersburg. It was founded in October 1905 and became the focal point for the general strike of that month.
- Started by the Union of Railway workers on 7 October 1905 with demands for political concessions and improved working conditions, the strike spread across the Empire.
- Unrest was not limited to the towns. In January and February 1906, uprisings took place in Kursk and the Volga regions. From October 1905 to August 1906, there was sporadic revolt in areas as diverse as the Baltic provinces to the Caucuses.

## The October Manifesto

The autocracy's response, prompted by **Count Witte**, was to issue the **October Manifesto** which bought the autocracy time.

- It granted a constitution and a **Duma** (parliament) with an extended franchise. It also promised to extend civil liberties.
- The result was to split the liberal opposition. Those in the opposition who accepted the government's proposals became known as **Octobrists**. Those who wished for further reform, such as a constituent assembly with far-reaching powers along western lines, became known as **Kadets**.
- In dividing the opposition and winning back the full support of the Army, the autocracy achieved its aim and made restoration of order by force possible.
- There was sporadic, continued defiance from the strikers – in December 1905 in Moscow there was a brief uprising which was suppressed by the Army.
- On 3 December 1905 the St Petersburg Soviet was closed down by the authorities. The government moved to suppress further unrest, having split the Revolution's supporters with the October Manifesto.

## Limited political reform

- A loan from France of 2,250 million francs secured the autocracy's financial position and the return of the army from Manchuria made possible the widespread clampdown on revolutionaries. 2,930 of those accused of being revolutionaries were executed between 1905–09.
- The **Fundamental Laws**, issued in April 1906, revealed that the autocracy was willing to accept only limited political reform. Included in the proposals were: a limited and unbalanced suffrage, the possibility of government by decree and no ministerial responsibility.
- The weakness of the Duma was highlighted by the premature dissolution of both its first (May–July 1906) and second (March–June 1907)

meetings, and by the passing of a new **Electoral Law** in June 1907. This altered the suffrage further in favour of groups loyal to the autocracy. The new law proposed that one deputy's vote was worth the equivalent of each of the following groups' votes: 230 landowners, 1,000 businessmen, 15,000 urban middle-class people, 60,000 peasants or 125,000 urban working class. These figures alone give a clear indication of the mistrust felt by the autocracy towards the proletariat.

- Although the third (1907–12) and fourth (1912–16) Dumas were more conciliatory towards the state, by 1911 the alliance between the autocracy and its supporters in the Octobrist Party had broken down.

## Stolypin and agrarian reform

The autocracy's response was repression with limited reform.

- Although land redistribution was not entertained, redemption payments were abolished from 1 November 1907 and the concept of a property-owning peasantry was turned into reality by **Stolpin's agrarian reforms**, introduced in November 1906.
- The effects of the reforms were not consistent across the Empire. In the south and west of the Empire, there was more of a move out of the villages, but in other areas change was slow.
- By 1915 only 22% of peasant households had individual land ownership. Further reform in 1910 which attempted to strengthen capitalism in the countryside, by making individual land ownership compulsory in some cases, came to little.
- Not only was there attempted reform on the issue of land holding, the legal status of the peasantry was raised in October 1906 and educational facilities were made more widely available in 1908.
- The assassination of Stolypin in 1911 ended the limited reforms of the autocracy.
- From 1907–11 there was little unrest. Social reform had given the working class the right to form unions in 1906 and insurance against accident in 1912.
- However, the shooting of around 200 strikers at the **Lena gold fields** in 1912 signalled a further outbreak of unrest.
- In 1914 strikes swept across the Empire from the oil wells of Baku to the Putilov factory in St Petersburg.

## The First World War

On declaration of war in 1914, most parties in opposition to the Tsar were prepared to put aside their domestic quarrels and to support the government. The defeat of Germany became the priority even for the revolutionary **Plekhanov** and for many in the largest left-wing movement, the **Socialist Revolutionaries** (the SRs). However, the war was to have important repercussions for the autocracy.

How to Pass AS Modern World History

- Widespread support for the autocracy ebbed away with the impact of growing economic hardship caused by inflation, which led to prices rising four times from 1914–17.
- The consequence was that the rouble had lost two-thirds of its pre-war value by 1917.
- Another destabilising factor was the failure of the Russian Army. From the start of the war the Germans proved themselves to be better organised and equipped.
- The Russian Army suffered a series of devastating defeats which began at **Tannenberg** in August 1914.
- In 1915 the Russian army retreated out of Poland at a cost of over a million men during the German offensive in **Galicia**.
- This was compounded in 1916 by the appointment of the allegedly pro-German Boris Sturmer as Chief of the Cabinet, and further military defeats.
- In June 1916, the **Brusilov Offensive** was launched by the Russian Army. Initially, the Austrian army was pushed back along a 300-mile front, but the arrival of German reinforcements signalled the end of any advance. The Russians failed to take their objectives of Kovel or Lemberg and the heavy losses led to discontent and demoralisation.

## Tsar, Empress and Rasputin

- On 5 September 1915, the Grand Duke Nicholas Nicolaievich was relieved of supreme command of the armed forces and his post was taken by the Tsar, Nicholas II. This had important consequences in that the Tsar's absence left the government at the mercy of the Empress Alexandra.
- Her German nationality and obvious hostility to the Duma, coupled with her fascination for the monk **Gregory Rasputin**, brought the government into considerable disrepute.
- Her fascination grew partly out of a reliance on Rasputin's healing powers. Nicholas II's son and heir, the **Tsarevich Alexis**, suffered from haemophilia. Rasputin, more than any doctor, seemed to be able to stem the boy's bleeding. However, his influence over the Empress and the royal family as a result of his skill was to cause much unease.
- In November 1916, the Duma met and the leaders attacked the 'dark forces' in the government.
- Unrest on the home front was caused by growing food shortages and exasperation with the war.
- Opposition groups within the Duma pressed for reform and Rasputin was murdered in December 1916.

# Assessment: Russia c. 1900–16

**Questions in the style of AQA (Unit 1)**

**Q 1 Study the following extract from the October Manifesto (Russia, 1905):**

> We ask the government
> - to grant to the population the right of free citizenship
> - to establish as an unbreakable rule that no law shall go into force without its confirmation by the State Duma ...

**Q    a With reference to Russia after 1905, explain the term 'State Duma'.** (3)

**How to answer this question**

You should recognise the source and the quote from it. The question is asking you to explain the powers and limitations of the Duma in the context of the source. Here is an example of an extract from an answer to this question. Note the attempt to refer to the source.

> The 'State Duma' was limited in its powers despite the claims of the October Manifesto that no law could be passed without its 'confirmation' by the Duma. Increasingly, Nicholas II and his ministers restricted the powers of the Duma to make laws. The Third and Fourth Dumas in particular lacked power to challenge the autocracy.

**Q    b Why did Nicholas II agree to the October Manifesto?** (7)

**How to answer this question**

This needs a straightforward, short, analytical answer. You should plan your key points of argument and prioritise them. You must show that you have reached a conclusion in response to the question.

Here are two arguments that you could put into your plan:
1  The most important reason for issuing the October Manifesto was that Nicholas II accepted that such a measure was necessary to protect the autocracy.
2  He agreed to the proposals so as to relieve pressure on the autocracy, to buy time, to divide the opposition and to ensure the support of the Army.

Q     c How far reaching was political reform in Russia in the period
      1905–14?                                                                (15)

## How to answer this question

This is a question which demands an analytical answer. You need to make a
very clear judgement about the extent of political reform in the period.
These are examples of lines of argument which you might use.
- Political reform was limited in extent because of the inability of the
  autocracy to reform without undermining itself.
- Despite the promises of 1905, political reform was minimal, the regime
  resorting to limited social reform and repression.

You should ensure that you cover the following topics:
- the October Manifesto and the Fundamental Laws
- the Dumas and electoral reform
- Stolypin and the emergence of revolutionary opposition.

Here is an extract from an attempt at this question. The candidate has
answered the question directly and has made a judgement. There is also a
good use of evidence.

---

Political reform was limited because of the contradiction between autocracy
and reform. Instead, the autocracy turned to repression, some 2000 people
being executed between 1905–08. Similarly, once secure in power, the
autocracy went back on the promises of the October Manifesto. The
limitations of the Fundamental Laws, which Trotsky called 'the police whip
wrapped in the parchment of the constitution', were followed by the 1907
electoral law which reduced the opposition in the Third Duma to 19 Social
Democrats and 54 Kadets. Meanwhile, the government-supporting
Octobrists gained 154 seats and their allies on the right another 97 seats.

---

## Questions in the style of OCR (Unit 3)

Q     2 a Examine the problems faced by Nicholas II in the period
      1906–17.                                                                (30)

## How to answer this question

To answer this question you need to identify some of the problems faced
by Nicholas II. Below is a list of the problems you might consider:
- the growth of an urban-based working class
- widespread dislike of the Empress and Rasputin
- the growth of opposition movements
- defeats in the Russo-Japanese War (1904–5) and the First World War
  (1914–17).

Note when answering a question like this that the specified period is important. Therefore your answer should not include any substantial explanation of the 1905 Revolution.

Here are a couple of examples of points you could put in your plan.

- Defeat in the wars discredited the autocracy because, in both cases, it linked the Tsar to failure. National humiliation and, in the First World War huge casualties, fuelled demands for political change.
- Dislike of the Empress and Rasputin was linked to the illness of the Tsarevich Alexis. However, rumour and gossip discredited the royal family and made possible a decline in support from key people.

Q    **b How important a reason for the decline in the popularity of the Tsar by late 1916 was Russia's involvement in the First World War?**                                                                (60)

**How to answer this question.**

The question offers the war as an explanation for the abdication of the Tsar. You are expected to explain the impact of the war and then discuss other factors.

Here the candidate attempts to link defeat in the war with a dislike of the Empress. The candidate also uses accurate detail.

---

Military disaster during the First World War led to the greater possibility of challenges to the autocracy. Nicholas also made some foolish mistakes which compounded his problems. Most obvious was his decision to become Supreme Commander of the Armed Forces in September 1915, relieving his uncle, Grand Duke Nicholas Nicolaievich, of the post. All military defeats which followed could be blamed on him. Nicholas' military role had important consequences in that the Tsar's absence left the government at the mercy of the Empress Alexandra. Her German nationality and obvious hostility to the Duma, coupled with her fascination for the monk Gregory Rasputin, brought the royal family and the Tsar into considerable disrepute. This disrepute was made worse in 1916 by the appointment of the allegedly pro-German Boris Sturmer as Chief of the Cabinet.

---

Q  **3 a Explain the extent to which Nicholas II's government reformed the Russian society and political system in the period 1906–14.**
                                                                    (30)

    **b How important a reason for the outbreak of revolution in 1905 was Russia's defeat in the Russo-Japanese War?**                (60)

# Section 2: The February and October Revolutions, 1917

## Abdication of the Tsar

On 9 January 1917, 140,000 workers in Petrograd staged a strike in memory of Bloody Sunday which was followed by further sporadic action.

- On 23 February 1917 another general strike took place. Two days later, the Tsar ordered troops to take whatever action was necessary to suppress such action.
- The response on 27 February 1917 was a general mutiny of the Army in Petrograd.
- On the same day, the members of the Cabinet resigned and the first meeting of the **Petrograd Soviet** took place.
- On 2 March 1917 the Tsar abdicated in favour of his brother Michael, who in turn abdicated in favour of the **Provisional Government** which was proclaimed the following day.

## The Provisional Government

- The first Prime Minister of the Provisional Government was **Prince Lvov** who ruled with the support of **Liberals** and **Kadets**.
- From February 1917 onwards, the government found itself sharing power with the Petrograd Soviet, which was dominated by SRs and Mensheviks. This led to the tense situation of '**Dual Power**'.
- The Soviet gave only conditional support to the Provisional Government. It accepted the government's right to rule, but only as long as it did not counteract what the Soviet interpreted as the spirit of the Revolution (e.g. improvement of living conditions or political freedoms).

## Continuation of the war

- Almost immediately, the government introduced a series of reforms including the right to strike, an amnesty for political prisoners and the abolition of capital punishment. However in continuing the war, the Provisional Government misunderstood one of the main causes of the February Revolution – the war's unpopularity.
- The Petrograd Soviet had demanded a revision of war aims and wanted to work towards a 'general democratic peace' without imperialist gains.
- In March 1917 it issued the *Order No. 1* which removed authority from military officers and placed Army administration in the hands of elected committees of soldiers. The order showed the government to be out of touch with the mass of the armed forces.
- Even more significant was the government's continuation of the military campaigns in search of a decisive victory. Although it superficially accepted the demands of the Soviet made in March that the war should

not be one of conquest but one of '**revolutionary defencism**' (that the war should be continued only with the objective of defending the Revolution and Russian motherland), this was never made clear.

- On 18 April 1917 the government pledged itself to the war against Germany in a note from the foreign minister Milyukov which promised to fight to a 'victorious end'.

## The Galician campaign

- In May the Kadet-based government fell and a coalition government was created which included two Mensheviks and the SR leaders **V. Chernov** and **A. Kerensky**.
- This new government continued with the war effort, Kerensky bringing new vigour to the post of Minister of War.
- In June and July 1917, the Russians launched the ill-fated Galician campaign. Despite initial gains, the Russian Army was thrown back onto the defensive. The series of battles which followed ended in August with the defeat of **General Kornilov's** forces at Riga. The result was further social unrest and a breakdown in army discipline.

## The issue of land

In the cities, rampant inflation angered the workers whilst in the country, expectations of land redistribution were not met by a government which found itself unable to enact radical legislation whilst the war continued. Land redistribution had become the peasantry's main expectation in the aftermath of the February Revolution. Throughout the early months of 1917, the government attempted to use force to stem the growing tide of land seizures.

## Lenin and the *April Thesis*

- Meanwhile, the Bolsheviks had begun to organise opposition to the Provisional Government based on the message of **unconditional opposition to the war.**
- On 3 April 1917, Lenin arrived at the Finland Station, Petrograd after travelling across Germany in a sealed train. The German High Command calculated that, by allowing Lenin to travel through Germany from Switzerland, the pro-Ally government would be undermined.
- The involvement of socialists and Mensheviks in the government from May onwards associated them with continuation of the war. This contrasted with the support the Bolsheviks gained from opposing the war.
- The *April Thesis*, which was drawn up by Lenin, took an uncompromising stance on the issue. It brought the party a tenfold increase in member-ship, to around 250,000 members by October.

The main points of the *April Thesis* were as follows.

How to Pass AS Modern World History

- The SRs and Mensheviks were attacked for their collaboration with the 'imperialist' government of Prince Lvov.
- It promised an end to the war and no support for the Provisional Government.
- It went on to guarantee government by the soviets, the immediate seizure of all land and the nationalisation of industry.
- It was a comprehensive manifesto for change, promising also the abolition of army, bureaucracy and police, and the end of parliamentary government.

The *April Thesis* appealed to many of those who took part in demonstrations against the Galician campaign, including the Kronstadt sailors who led the so called '**July Days**' uprising. This support became crucial in the Bolsheviks' seizure of power, the Petrograd garrison being unwilling to prevent the seizure of power in October. There is no doubt that the slogans of '**Bread, Peace and Land**' won huge support.

### The Kornilov affair

- The response of the new coalition government led by Kerensky was to turn many against the Bolsheviks by accurately accusing them of accepting finance from Germany.
- Lenin was temporarily forced to flee to Finland but the Bolsheviks benefited soon after from the threat of a counter-revolution led by **General Kornilov**. He was the Commander in Chief of the Russian Army under the Provisional Government.
- In August 1917, he was persuaded by other right-wing elements in the army of the necessity of a military coup d'etat.
- Acting with the support of many officers of the army, Kornilov indicated his intention on 27 August to march on Petrograd and restore order.
- To defend the capital, Kerensky armed the soviet and workers' militia, which included many Bolsheviks. The threat from Kornilov was removed by the actions of the railway workers.

### Growing Bolshevik success

- From January to October the real wage of the average worker had been reduced by 57%, in 1917 the rouble having only 10% of its value in 1914.
- Growing unemployment as a result of shortages in raw materials, coupled with increasing governmental intervention on the side of employers in disputes resulted in the election of a Bolshevik majority to the Petrograd Soviet on 31 August.
- Bolshevik success was not limited to Petrograd: on 5 September they won a majority in the Moscow Soviet and later in the same month they won elections to the Duma in the same city.

- The response of the government on 14 September was to attempt to form some political consensus via the **Democratic Convention** (which was intended as a pre-Parliament to pave the way for a democratically-elected Constituent Assembly). However, the exercise backfired, as the Bolsheviks walked out and Kerensky was forced to include Kadets in his Cabinet – who were perceived by many on the left as counter-revolutionaries.
- All these events encouraged Lenin, who argued strongly that, given the European situation, the time was right for revolution.

## Economic collapse

The war created the conditions in which the Bolshevik slogans found the ready support of a population suffering from the effects of a collapsing economy. Although the support for the Bolsheviks was not a majority one, it was a strategically important one.

- In Petrograd and the other major cities, the workers suffered increasing deprivation as the war progressed. During 1917, bread prices rose as the supply dried up, whilst inflation reduced the rouble to 10% of its 1914 value.
- Against this background of economic collapse, the employers used a policy of lockouts, partly due to raw material shortages but also because it was an effective weapon to deal with labour unrest.
- The result was increasing unemployment; over 60,000 workers were sacked in Moscow from late July to September. It was from the discontented working class that the Bolsheviks recruited their core support. This support included the 10,000-strong Red Guard in Petrograd and those who elected a Bolshevik majority at the Second All-Russian Congress of Soviets in October.

## Run up to the October Revolution

The Bolsheviks were best placed to carry out a revolution through their dominance of the soviet and, in particular, the Petrograd Soviet Military Defence Committee set up on 9 October 1917.

- Through this institution, the Red Guard were armed and organised. The Red Guard had also been armed at the height of the Kornilov Crisis and had retained the weapons it had been given at that time.
- On 10 October, a meeting of the Bolshevik Central Committee in Petrograd decided on the course of armed uprising as proposed by the now present Lenin.
- There were significant doubts, raised by Kamenev and Zinoviev in particular, of the consequences of failure of what was ideologically a premature revolution.

It was **Lenin** who convinced the Bolsheviks that revolution was right

How to Pass AS Modern World History

within a European context. Uprisings abroad would bring socialist solidarity, which would support a Bolshevik revolution in Russia. Meanwhile they could concentrate on undertaking a revolution in the name of the working class. There were worries expressed that the Revolution would not be mirrored abroad and that it might not even find sympathy amongst a slogan-weary Russian working class.

The cause of armed insurgency was aided by the Petrograd Soviet's creation of the Military Revolutionary Committee on 16 October. Set up to co-ordinate the military defence of Petrograd in the case of a German attack, the effect was to provide the Bolsheviks with the means by which they could arm and organise the Red Guards. On 23 October, Trotsky visited the strategically important St Peter and Paul fortress in Petrograd and won the support of the soldiers whose guns protected the Winter Palace.

## The October Revolution

- Kerensky ordered that the Bolshevik press in Petrograd be seized and that the Aurora battleship stationed outside the Palace be put to sea. On 24 and 25 October, the Red Guards countered these orders and seized strategically important points, including the telegraph exchange and post offices.
- Kerensky fled Petrograd and the rest of his government was arrested after the Winter Palace had been taken on the night of the 25/26 October.
- Simultaneously, the Second Congress of Soviets met with a majority of 300 Bolsheviks and 90 left-wing SRs.
- As the Winter Palace was stormed, so the Mensheviks and right-wing SRs walked out of the Congress leaving Kamenev to pronounce the success of the Revolution in the name of the Soviets.

# Assessment: The February and October Revolutions, 1917

**Questions in the style of Edexcel (Unit 1)**

**Q 1 Study the sources below and then answer the following questions.**

**Source A** Adapted from the memoirs of a Bolshevik leader of the Kronstadt sailors in 1917. The memoirs were published in 1962.

> The July events took place quite spontaneously. The working class and the peasantry in soldiers' and sailors' greatcoats sensed that the Provisional Government was destroying the Revolution. Without waiting for any call, on 3 July they surged onto the streets on their own initiative. How did the Bolshevik Party react to this? On 2 and 3 July, it strove with all the influence it possessed to hold back the masses who followed it, but their collective will was so striking that on the evening of 4 July, the Party decided to put itself at the head of the unavoidable movement and, by introducing consciousness into its spontaneity, transfer it into a peaceful and organised armed demonstration.

**Source B** Adapted from G Katkov and H Shukman's *Lenin's Path to Power*, published in 1971.

> This point is of great importance. Soviet historians have tried to prove that neither Lenin nor the Bolshevik Central Committee had anything to do with preparing the July rising. In fact, with the usual deceit two members of the Central Committee addressed the mob, appealing for an end to the demonstration and a return to barracks. They were met with cries of 'Down with them' and 'All power to the Soviets!'. The Bolshevik Central Committee then decided to organise the 'spontaneous' demonstration.

**Source C** Adapted from *Ten days that Shook the World* by American journalist John Reed and published in 1926.

> As a result of the disastrous failure of the [July] rising, public opinion turned against the Bolsheviks and their leaderless hordes slunk back to the Viborg quarter. Then followed a savage hunt of Bolsheviks; hundreds were imprisoned, among them Trotsky, Madame Kollantei and Kamenev; Lenin and Zinoviev went into hiding; the Bolshevik papers were suppressed. Reactionaries raised the cry that the Bolsheviks were German agents, until people all over the world believed it. But the Provisional Government found itself unable to substantiate its accusations and one by one the Bolsheviks were released.

**Source D** Adapted from a letter written by Lenin to the Bolshevik Central Committee. Sent from Finland in September 1917.

> We shall fight, we are fighting against Kornilov, just as Kerensky's troops do, but we do not support Kerensky. On the contrary, we expose his weakness. There is a difference. A rather subtle difference, but it is highly essential and must not be forgotten ...We must campaign not so much directly against Kerensky as indirectly against him, by demanding a more and more active, truly revolutionary war against Kornilov, by drawing the masses in, by arousing them, by inflaming them (Kerensky is afraid of the masses, afraid of the people).

**Source E** Adapted from S Fitzpatrick's *The Russian Revolution, 1917–1932*, published in 1932.

> In September Lenin wrote from his hiding place in Finland urging the Bolshevik Party that the revolutionary movement had come. Delay would be fatal. Lenin's urging for immediate armed uprising was passionate but not entirely convincing to his colleagues in the leadership. Lenin did not return to take charge; surely he would have done so if he were really serious? When he did return to Petrograd, probably at the end of the first week of October, he stayed in hiding, isolated even from the Bolsheviks, and communicated with his Central Committee through a series of angry letters.

**Q** a Study Source A. According to this Source, why did the Bolshevik Party 'react' to the demands for demonstrations in Petrograd in July 1917? **(3)**

## How to answer this question

This question is asking you to show that you understand the author's point in the source about the relationship between the Bolsheviks and the working classes in July 1917.

**Q** b Study Source B and use your own knowledge. Explain what the demonstrators meant in 1917 by 'All power to the Soviets'. **(5)**

## How to answer this question

In your answer you should concentrate on the main issue in the question, that of the Soviets. You should refer to the source and your own knowledge when answering the question.

Here is an extract from an answer to this question. Note how the candidate has attempted to answer the question directly, has used his or her own knowledge and has referred to the source.

By July 1917 there was increased unrest as a result of the continuation of the war. Military defeat in the Galician campaign meant an increase in support for soldier soviets. As the source shows, many of the demonstrators were soldiers – they were encouraged to 'return to barracks'. The soldiers' soviets campaigned for an end to the war, hence the cry for power to be given to them.

**Q** c Study Sources B and C. To what extent do these sources agree with the view that the Bolsheviks were not responsible for the 'July Days'? (5)

## How to answer this question

You must ensure that you use both sources to answer this question. You should also try to quote from both sources (although you should make sure that your quotes are short and to the point). The question demands that you come to a conclusion and so it is important that you make a brief plan before you start.

The plan should be based around an argument put in response to the question and should outline how the sources agree and disagree with the view that 'the Bolsheviks were not responsible for the "July Days" '.

Here are some key points to put in your plan. These can become the main points in the introduction to your answer:
- To an extent, the sources support the stated view. They show that the Bolshevik Central Committee did not start the disorder.
- However, Bolsheviks had a significant effect on what happened during the July Days.

**Q** d Study Sources D and E. How useful are these sources to an historian studying Lenin's authority in the Bolshevik Party in September 1917? (5)

## How to answer this question

This is a question about the utility of the evidence. For advice on how to answer this type of question you should refer to Chapter 2.

**Q** e Study Sources A and D and use your own knowledge. Do you agree that support for the Bolsheviks differed between July and September 1917? Give your reasons. (12)

## How to answer this question

In this question you are being asked to make a judgement based on the sources and your own knowledge. It is important that you use both. You should try and prioritise your reasons for a change in Bolshevik support.

These are some topics you might refer to:
- the worsening economic situation
- repression
- creation of the Red Guard
- the aftermath of the Kornilov Affair
- the increasing impact of Bolshevik propaganda amongst strategically important groups
- the unpopularity of Kerensky's government due to failure in war and the German advance.

Try to blend the information from the sources with your own knowledge. Here is an extract from an answer to the question.

> Support for the Bolsheviks varied between urban and rural areas. However support for the Bolsheviks grew as a result of increasing industrial unrest and as a result of worsening economic conditions in the major cities. This was done by what Lenin describes in Source D as 'drawing the masses in, by arousing them'. Increasing government intervention on the side of employers in disputes and Bolshevik campaigning resulted in the election of a Bolshevik majority to the Petrograd Soviet on 31 August and on 5 September they won a majority in the Moscow Soviet.

## Further question in the style of AQA (Unit 1)

Q 2 **Using the sources A–E above and your own knowledge explain why revolution took place in October 1917.** (12)

# Section 3: The Bolshevik consolidation of power, 1917–24

## Dealing with opposition

- The new Bolshevik government had many enemies and immediately had to use force to counter the threats to their position.
- Forces loyal to the Provisional Government under General Pëtr **Krasnov** were defeated in and around Petrograd from 28–30 October 1917.
- Moscow was taken by the Bolsheviks on 2 November.
- On 27 October, the Bolsheviks began to close down the opposition press. Such were the continuing doubts of many in the Bolshevik leadership about their own ability to carry through the Revolution without support of others on the left, that five members of the Central Committee (CC) resigned over the muzzling of the press, including Kamenev.
- The Bolsheviks were not in a strong enough position to prevent the prearranged elections to the **Constituent Assembly** on 12 November. Where the peasants' support lay was very clear with the right-wing SRs receiving 17.1 million votes (41%) and 370 seats; the Bolsheviks gaining only 9.8 million votes (23.5%) and 168 seats.
- The Assembly first met on 5 January 1918 but was disbanded a day later by Bolshevik troops on Lenin's orders.

## Decrees and policy innovation

Decrees were immediately passed on peace and land, and an interim government – the Bolshevik-only **Council of People's Commissars** – was set up. The land decree ordered the immediate breaking up of large estates and distribution of that land to the peasants.

- In November 1917 the legal system was abolished and on 15 November workers were given control over the factories.
- The party-dominated Supreme Council of the National Economy (*Vesenkha*) was set up on 5 December to co-ordinate and impose state control over the economy.
- In mid December, the banks were nationalised by decree and on the 28 January 1918, the national debt was repudiated and all foreign loans cancelled.
- The Bolsheviks launched their much-heralded attack on the Orthodox Church and religion in the **Decree on the Separation of Church and State**, which was published in January 1918. Its main aim was to confiscate all Church property and place it in state hands.

These decrees went some way to meeting the aspirations of their supporters and gave the Bolsheviks a base of support which was to prove invaluable during the Civil War. The support of the working class was consolidated by the numerous decrees on factory control, such as that of

14 November 1917 which handed over the factories to worker committees. The Bolsheviks immediately enacted legislation on women which delivered the long-promised emancipation. Lenin had been a long-standing advocate of women's rights and was strongly supportive of the Women's Department set up under the supervision of feminist **Alexandra Kollontai**. The legislation of 1918–20 reflected her agenda.

- Up to the end of 1918, women won the right to vote, were given **equal pay**, given **paid maternity leave** and access to **divorce** amongst other rights.
- In 1920 women were given the right to free **abortion**.
- Women also benefited from the labour legislation which, amongst other things, banned night work for women.
- This and other decrees were brought together in the **Labour Code of 1922** which had the aim of providing workers with rights in the workplace.

## Brest Litovsk

- As it had promised, the new government immediately opened peace negotiations with Germany.
- Although Trotsky attempted a number of tactics to divert the Germans from their demands before peace could be signed, they were unyielding. With German troops advancing on Petrograd in February 1918 the Bolshevik government was forced to accept humiliating terms for peace, which were signed at Brest Litovsk on 3 March.
- The treaty was opposed by many within the Bolshevik leadership, including Bukharin and Dzerzhinsky, but Lenin and eventually Trotsky accepted peace at any cost.
- The Bolsheviks signed away **Poland** and the **Baltic States** to German control, whilst accepting the independence of the Ukraine, Georgia and Finland. Such loss was too much for the left-wing SRs who ended any remaining links they had with the Bolsheviks, now called the **Communists**.

## The Red Terror

To protect itself and to counter opposition the government created **Cheka** on 7 December 1917.

- The organisation was led by the ruthless **Felix Dzerzhinsky**. It acted as the new government's secret police and terror organisation.
- At the Vth Congress of Soviets in July 1918, there was considerable tension between the Communists and left-wing SRs who shouted down Trotsky and proceeded to assassinate the German ambassador in an attempt to provoke war.
- They capped this by arresting Dzerzhinsky on 6 July.
- The Communist response was swift – the left-wing SRs were removed wholesale from the Congress and a right-wing SR uprising in Yaroslav in

late July was viciously repressed. This signalled the start of a Red Terror at the hands of Cheka.

## The Red Terror takes hold

All legal restraint was ignored, to be replaced by '**revolutionary conscience**'.

- This meant that people were to be tried by revolutionary tribunals which were, in reality, Communist courts.
- In response to the assassination attempt of the Petrograd Cheka Chief **Uritsky** on 30 August 1918, over 500 hostages were shot by Kronstadt sailors.
- The same day saw the attempted assassination of Lenin by Fanya Kaplan.
- The Communists responded in September by passing two important decrees relating to the Terror. The first allowed the taking of hostages who would be executed for further attempts on Communist lives. This was followed by a decree which proposed an intensified terror against the 'class enemies' of Communism.
- These decrees legally recognised what was already happening, e.g. in Petrograd on 31 August Zinoviev ordered the execution of 512 hostages.
- There were other methods used to suppress opposition apart from assassination and terror – forced labour camps were created in 1918 and by 1920 there were around 50,000 people in these camps.
- It is difficult to know how many people were imprisoned but it could be as high as 200,000.
- The significance of the Red Terror is that it cowed the population and removed effective internal opposition to Communist rule.

## The Civil War 1918–20.

- The Bolshevik Revolution faced considerable danger from a number of armed opposition groups. To counter the threat, the **Red Army** was created by Trotsky on 23 February 1918 and organised into a highly effective military organisation.
- The first threat to the Red Army came in the east where a Czech Army succeeded in May 1918 in capturing **Ekaterinburg**, and Kazan in August.
- There was also considerable threat from Denikin's army in the south. The isolation of the Reds was shown by the creation of numerous governments, including those set up in the summer by the former allies Chernov in the Volga region and Chaikovsky in Archangel.
- These governments were eventually subsumed by a more conservative government led by **Admiral Kolchak**, who was pronounced Supreme Ruler of Russia in November 1918.

To make matters worse, there was considerable foreign intervention in the Civil War. The British landed troops in Murmansk in March 1918 and a whole host of nationalities (including American and Japanese troops) landed in the Far East throughout the rest of the year. Although their stated aim was to protect their interests and prevent weapons falling into German hands, there was considerable fighting between them and the Red Army in the spring of 1919. It was ended only with British and American withdrawal from Archangel in September and Murmansk in October 1919. In the Ukraine, the German army overran the country in March 1918. After the November armistice, the French occupied Odessa, only to be expelled in April 1919.

The situation for the Communists seemed critical in 1919 with their Army facing enemies on numerous fronts.

- In the east, Kolchak's armies had taken Perm and Ufa, but this was the limit of their advance. By November 1919, the Red Army had taken Omsk and forced the White Army to retreat to Irkutsk.
- Much prized for its oil, the region of Southern Russia was a target for the Red Army but their attempts to fill the vacuum left by the retreating German and Austrian Armies were foiled by General Denikin in January 1919. The Whites then took to the offensive and had captured Kiev by September 1919, but they too were forced into retreat in December. In March 1920, Denikin turned his command over to General Wrangel.
- From April to October 1920 the Red Army was distracted by war with Poland which attempted to overrun the Ukraine. The war was ended by the preliminary **Treaty of Riga** of October 1920 (the formal treaty being signed in March 1921) which left the Ukraine to the Russian government.
- This freed the Red Army to pursue Wrangel's demoralised Army, which was finally evacuated from the Crimea in November 1920.

## Why the Reds won

There were significant differences between the two sides which were to prove crucial in the war's outcome.

- Most importantly, the **Red Army** was far **better organised** and more co-ordinated than its enemy.
- Even the appointment of Kolchak as Central Commander in November 1918 had little impact – the Whites failed to copy the **single command structure** created by Trotsky for the Red Army in 1918.
- The Whites were **politically divided** with groups as diverse as the reactionary elements led by Kolchak to the short-lived socialist government at Ufa led by Chernov. This was in contrast to the ideologically motivated and policed Red Army.
- There were also **geographical factors** which helped the Reds to victory. They were in control of a centralised area whilst their opponents were spread over a disparate area with poor communications.

## War Communism

The Civil War had caused severe economic problems which, with the ideological aspirations of the Bolsheviks, helped to shape the policy of **War Communism**. The loss of territory and the collapse of the currency dictated stringent measures.

- On 19 February 1918, all **land was nationalised** and a system of requisitioning (taking by force) the peasant surplus was introduced by the summer. Although a success in terms of the fact that the urban population was fed, requisitioning caused significant rural unrest. The situation in the country was desperate as many peasants withheld grain and famine struck many areas.
- Meanwhile, in June 1918 all **factories were nationalised**, Vesenkha taking a leading role in organising industrial production.
- Industrial discipline was tightened with strict penalties being introduced in May 1920 for absenteeism.
- The party too was reorganised, with ever increasing discipline replacing internal debate. At the VIIIth Party Congress in March 1919 the central decision-making body, the **Politburo**, was formally recognised. However, greater centralisation of the decision-making process was opposed by many within the party and dissent was rife.

## Kronstadt and the New Economic Policy

- From February to March 1921, the sailors of Kronstadt Fortress in Petrograd (who had been in the vanguard of the Revolution in 1917) revolted against the government and demanded the end to War Communism and free elections.
- The mutiny was crushed by the Red Army but forced the government into full retreat. At the Xth Party Congress in March 1921, the **New Economic Policy (NEP)** was presented by Lenin and adopted by the delegates. It signalled the end of War Communism and the requisitioning of grain.
- The banks, the transport system and large-scale industry were to remain in state hands but small-scale businesses could operate again on the free market.
- It was a pragmatic step back from socialism but, to force the NEP through Congress, dissent and debate within the Party was abolished in March 1921. That the NEP was an unpopular innovation amongst Party members is without doubt, but the **banning of dissent** imposed on the Party at the Xth Party Congress ended any effective opposition to it.
- The NEP gave the regime breathing space as its introduction helped to stimulate the required economic growth and defused the simmering unrest in the countryside.

## Nationalities question

The nationalities issue was one which threatened the new Communist state.

- Independent states were declared in the peripheral nations of the old Empire, in line with Lenin's Declaration of November 1917. However, such a trend increasingly became a threat to the government with states such as Georgia declaring her independence in mid-1918 and electing a Menshevik government.
- As it became apparent that the rest of Europe's working classes were not going to rise up in support of the Russian Revolution, so policy changed.
- In 1921, Soviet governments were set up in Georgia and Armenia and in March 1922 these governments were combined with that of Azerbaijan to form the Transcaucasian **Socialist Soviet Republic**, despite fierce opposition in Georgia.
- On 30 December 1922, the **USSR** – the **Union of Socialist Soviet Republics** – was brought into being.

# Assessment: The Bolshevik consolidation of power, 1917–24

## Questions in the style of Edexcel (Unit 2)

**Q** **What was Trotsky's contribution to the Bolshevik victory in the Civil War, 1918–21?** **(15)**

### How to answer this question

This question focuses on Trotsky and is asking you to explain his contribution in detail. You should show a clear understanding of events during the Civil War and might also compare Trotsky with his White counterparts.

Here is an extract from an answer to this question. The section is about Trotsky's organisation of the Red Army.

> Trotsky's significance was as leader of the Red Army. Most importantly, the Red Army was far better organised and more co-ordinated than its enemy. The differences in organisation between the two sides were to prove crucial to the war's outcome. Even the appointment of Kolchak as Central Commander in November 1918 had little impact; the Whites failed to copy the single command structure created by Trotsky for the Red Army in 1918. The Whites were politically divided with groups as diverse as the reactionary elements led by Kolchak to the short-lived socialist government at Ufa led by Chernov. This was a contrast to the ideologically motivated and policed Red Army. By 1920, the Army had only five million men. Their resolve was stiffened by 180,000 political commissars whose task was to ensure loyalty to the government.

**Q** **Explain why the White armies were so divided and ineffective.**

**(15)**

### How to answer this question

This question requires you to present an analytical answer. You must plan a line of argument which includes a prioritisation of the factors.

Here are some examples of points you might make in your plan:
- The White armies were divided because they were made up of many different anti-Bolshevik groups. Also important were the geographical divisions which made a coherent campaign difficult.
- The White Armies were ineffective because they lacked the strategically

important support of the peasantry, some nationalities and the urban working class.

## Further questions in the style of Edexcel (Unit 2)

Q 2 a In what ways did Soviet society change in the period
1918–41?                                                                  (15)
   b Why, and with what results, did Lenin introduce the NEP?     (15)

Q 3 a Describe how the Communists consolidated power in the
Soviet Union by 1924.                                                (15)
   b Explain why the Whites lost the Civil War.                        (15)

# Section 4: Stalin's rise to power and collectivisation

## Lenin's death, 1924

The struggle to succeed Lenin took place against the backdrop of an ideological debate about the future nature of the Soviet economy. The leading contenders to replace Lenin each had their sources of power

- **Stalin**. In May 1922 Stalin was appointed as General Secretary of the Communist Party, a post which placed him in charge of the Secretariat. The significance of this post was that Stalin controlled the appointments of Party members to positions of power and it allowed him to dominate Party congresses. Stalin cleverly underplayed the significance of his position and he was not considered the automatic successor to Lenin. Few in the Party perceived the potential danger posed by Stalin, although Lenin wrote in his Testament (1922) that 'Comrade Stalin ... has unlimited authority concentrated in his hands, and I am not sure whether he will be capable of using that authority with enough caution'.
- **Leon Trotsky** held influence in the Party as Commissar for War. As the creator of the Red Army, he was widely recognised as the victor of the Civil War. However Trotsky had only joined the Bolsheviks in 1917. Previously he had been a Menshevik. Trotsky's weakness was that he did not have the same power base as Stalin. Because he was Lenin's assumed heir this made him vulnerable to political attack. In 1923 Stalin joined with leading Bolsheviks Kamenev and Zinoviev to oppose Trotsky.

## Socialism in one country versus permanent revolution

By 1927, the New Economic Policy had fulfilled its primary aim of restoring industry to the production levels of 1913, yet the Soviet economy lagged further behind those of the West. There were conflicting views within the Communist Party about the future of the economy and how a surplus in agricultural produce could be extracted from the peasantry:

- **Proposals associated with Nikolai Bukharin**. The peasantry should be allowed to prosper by using modern production methods. Through this, excess grain would be produced which could be sold abroad. This would provide the capital for investment in industry. Although these proposals would mean only the gradual introduction of a socialist state, it had at its cornerstone the alliance between peasant and urban working class as envisaged by Lenin in 1917.
- **'Left opposition' led by Leon Trotsky**. Trotsky argued that the Revolution would only be safe when the whole world had become communist and it was the duty of the Party to promote 'permanent revolution'. Trotsky argued for an end to the NEP and rapid industrialisation. He believed that the peasantry should shoulder the

burden of rapid industrialisation through taxation, procurements of grain and depressed living standards. The resources generated by collectivisation of farming should be redirected into heavy industry.

- **Stalin's views**. Stalin allied himself, for political reasons, with Bukharin as Trotsky was his most obvious rival for the leadership of the Party. However, by 1928 he was also promoting the idea of '**socialism in one country**'. Stalin believed that economic progress required the more direct methods used during the Civil War.

## The defeat of Trotsky

In 1925 Trotsky was removed as Commissar for War. The next year Stalin defeated Trotsky politically and in December 1927 Trotsky and Zinoviev were exiled by the XVth Party Congress. Almost immediately, Stalin and his supporters began to assert an independent line from Bukharin by pressing the Central Committee to allow the requisitioning of grain by force. The reasons for this were partly ideological and partly a consequence of an impending crisis in agriculture. An excuse for action came in the shape of the so-called '**requisitioning crisis**' of late 1927. Rising prices in consumer goods due to scarcity led peasants to sell less grain as there was little use for cash, especially as grain prices were falling. By December 1927 the state agencies which bought grain from the peasantry had only managed to buy 50% of the previous year's total. To most activists at the XVth Party Congress, this was evidence of deliberate hoarding by the **kulaks** (rich peasants) and the best excuse possible to reassert Bolshevik control.

## The defeat of Bukharin

In January 1928, Stalin ordered requisitioning of grain by force and the arrest of dissenting peasants under Article 107 of the Criminal Code (which forbad speculation). This was to become known as the **Urals-Siberian method** and it destroyed any confidence the peasantry had in the state. It also opened up a rift between Stalin and Bukarin, who opposed forced requisitioning of grain. Despite the demands of the July Central Committee plenum (meeting) to end the practice, it continued apace into the spring of 1929. The right was increasingly discredited in Party organisations and institutions. In December 1928, Bukharin was forced to resign as editor of *Pravda* following the publication in September of the article *Notes of an economist* which implied criticism of Stalin and his methods. He was finally discredited in November 1929, by being expelled from the Central Committee.

## Collectivisation

- The process of collectivisation was already underway and Stalin claimed in his article of 7 November 1929, *Year of the Great Breakthrough*, that the time was ripe for an all-out offensive against rural capitalism.

- The following month was marked by celebrations of Stalin's 50th birthday (this point marking the beginning of the '**cult of the personality**') and a speech on 27 December in which he explicitly called for the liquidation of the kulaks.
- On 5 January 1930, the Central Committee announced the programme for the forced collectivisation of agriculture. By spring, some 30 million hectares were to have been collectivised, the process to be undertaken by 25,000 Party activists, joined by around 125,000 workers and troops.
- In February 1930 a decree was passed which gave the go-ahead for the elimination of the kulak class. By the beginning of March the countryside had been thrown into complete turmoil. In two months it was claimed over 10 million households had been forced into collectives.

## Turmoil in the countryside

Collectivisation took place at the hands of 25,000 Party activists formed into '**collectivisation brigades**' who were more than willing to implement what they saw as a renewal and a completion of the Revolution of 1917. In many areas, such as the Ukraine and the Caucuses, there was widespread resistance to collectivisation. Across the Soviet Union peasants slaughtered their livestock rather than let it fall into the hands of the collectivisation brigades. Around one-fifth of the country's cattle and a quarter of the country's total livestock was slaughtered in the first two months of 1930 alone.

Such was the opposition and turmoil, Stalin ordered a temporary respite in *Dizzy with success*, printed in March 1930. This article blamed the excesses of collectivisation on overzealous local officials. In addition, it ordered the re-establishment of the principle that farmers could join the kolkhozes voluntarily and could leave if they so wished. The stampede out of the kolkhozes left a rump of only 6 million households collectivised in June, as opposed to around 15 million in March. The rationale for the article was to ensure the harvest was sown in the spring, which it duly was.

At the XVIth Party Congress in June 1930, Stalin again signalled that collectivisation was central to the process of building a socialist state in the Soviet Union, and the forced process of collectivisation was restarted. From the summer of 1930, purges of the agricultural bureaucracy became commonplace. In September over 1000 Party members, including the former Minister of Food, N A Kondratiev, were arrested and accused of belonging to the anti-collectivisation (and completely fictitious) 'Toiling Peasant Party'.

## Consequences

Collectivisation was undertaken with little planning and kolkhozes were often run by members of collectivisation brigades with little or no experience of agricultural affairs.

- Because of fine weather, the harvest of 1930 was unexpectedly good, in all 77 million tons of grain were produced (out of which the state still only managed to take 22 million tons). This output was the exception to the rule, however, and was to provoke considerable problems later on when the state demanded quotas based on 1930 figures.
- Across the Soviet Union there was turmoil on an unprecedented scale. At a conservative estimate, over 2.5 million kulaks alone were exiled in 1930–31.
- After the initial wave of destruction came **famine**. From late 1931 to mid-1934 the state continued to demand high quotas of grain and other foodstuffs whilst hunger spread across the Soviet Union. Hardest hit was the **Ukraine** where the absurdly high quota of 7.7 million tons of grain (36% of the total harvest) to be handed over to the state was set in 1931. In 1932, the Ukraine was set a quota of 6.6 million tons, yet only 4.7 million was collected. In the Ukraine, perhaps as many as 5 million people died between 1931–34.
- The peasantry was made subject to a series of harsh decrees which had the intention of controlling all aspects of rural life and closely resembled serfdom. In 1931, all peasants became liable to spend 6 days a year mending the roads. Similar decrees, passed in 1932, banned trade in the kolkhozes until quotas had been met, reintroduced internal passports and passed a sentence of execution for theft of kolkhoz property.
- By the end of 1934, some 70% of households were collectivised, the figure rising to 90% by 1936 through the imposition of high taxes and quotas on those who remained outside the system.

## The role of arts

In the early 1920s the communists did not control all aspects of art. However by 1929 Soviet culture was dominated by the **Association of Proletarian Writers** (RAPP). Then, all Russian culture became part of the Five Year Plans. Stalin viewed writers as 'engineers of the human soul' and in 1932 RAPP was closed down to be reorganised into the state-run **Union of Soviet Writers**. Of particular importance was **socialist realism**. Defined in the period 1932–34 and reflected in the works of writers such as Michael Sholokhov, socialist realism rejected the abstract or romantic as 'bourgeois'. Instead it defined as acceptable cultural expression which reflected the regime's ideological message. Another trend in culture was the re-emergence of Russian nationalism.

## The role of women

The revolution liberated Russian women (women became an important part of the workforce, e.g. a quarter of coal miners in 1939 were women) but the 1930s saw a return to more traditional attitudes towards women. The state's attitudes towards women and the family changed:

- After the revolution, decrees were passed which gave women equal rights in marriage. By the decree of 1936 called '**In Defence of Mother and Child**' this was now reversed.
- Divorce was now made much harder, abortion was banned, adultery and promiscuity were criminalised.
- The 1936 decree also set up extensive childcare provision to encourage women into work. The decree was part of a wider campaign to promote nuptiality. Those with small families or who were single were taxed, and medals were struck for women with five or more children.

# Assessment: Stalin's rise to power and collectivisation

## Questions in the style of Edexcel (Unit 3)

**Source A** Adapted from *The Russian Peasantry 1600–1930: The World the Peasants Made* by David Moon, 1999.

> Collectivisation was an all-out attack on the peasantry. Party officials were sent out from the cities to persuade or force peasants to join the new collective farms. The collectivisers also attacked village churches and implemented 'dekulakisation'. Most peasants held Stalin directly responsible for the ensuing chaos and disaster. Peasants rioted to stop the formation of collective farms, to free imprisoned kulaks or to defend their churches.

**Q 1 Study Source A.**
   **a What, according to Source A, were the peasants' attitudes towards collectivisation?** (5)

### How to answer this question

This question is asking you to interpret and use the source. You need to show a sound understanding of the motives of the peasants in opposing the introduction of the collective farms. Try not to write out an account of what the peasants did – use the source to back up a point of explanation. Here is an extract from an answer to this question.

> The peasants opposed collectivisation as a direct attack on their culture. They rejected the atheism of the Communists which, as Source A points out, went hand in hand with collectivisation. The peasants resisted and attempted to 'defend their churches'.

**Q b What arguments were used in the 1920s and 30s by those in favour of introducing collectivisation?** (7)

### How to answer this question

The question is asking you to give a developed explanation for the arguments in favour of collectivisation. Answers should focus on the ideological arguments in favour of collectivisation: the rejection of the NEP; socialism in one country; reaction to the procurement crisis; rekindling of the Revolution. You might also concentrate on the wish of Stalin to use collectivisation to control the countryside and the Nationalities.

**Q** c What was the impact of collectivisation on the Soviet people in the period 1930–39? (18)

**How to answer this question**

To achieve the highest marks, you need to make a judgement which you sustain throughout your answer. There are many areas you might focus on, including standards of living in the countryside, migration, famine, the kulaks, agricultural production, the extent of mechanisation, food supplies to the cities, forced labour, different nationalities within the Soviet Union and the impact on the communists.

**Further question in the style of Edexcel (Unit 3)**

**Q** 2 a Describe how Stalin isolated his rivals in the struggle to succeed Lenin in the years 1924–29. (15)

b Why did Stalin order the collectivisation of agriculture from 1928? (15)

# Section 5: Soviet industrialisation and the purges

## Industrialisation

- In May 1927, Britain broke off diplomatic relations with the Soviet Union, and poor relations with the outside world generally convinced most communists that the threat of invasion was real.
- From late 1926 the state had been involved in heavy capital projects, including the vast **Volga-Don Canal** and the **Turksib railway** line linking Siberia to Turkestan. At the XVth Party Congress in December 1927 Stalin proclaimed the virtues of such schemes and further industrialisation to stave off the impending invasions.
- When this scare had receded another enemy was created, namely the mining engineers of the Shakhty region. In April 1928 a so-called 'conspiracy' was 'uncovered' and 50 engineers were placed on trial charged with wrecking.
- The pace of reform intensified with planning agencies competing with each other to produce plans for growth. In April 1929 a plan drawn up by the two foremost planning agencies, Gosplan and Vesenka, was adopted by the XVIth Party Congress. Setting quite fantastic targets, the **Five Year Plan** was backdated to October 1928 and set to run to mid-1933. By its terms, steel production was to rise from 4 million tons to 10.5 million tons between 1928–33 (the actual figure reached was 6 million tons).
- To power the new industries, the target for electricity production was 22 million kilowatt hours in 1933 as opposed to 5 million in 1928 (in the end 13.4 million kilowatt hours were achieved).

## The wreckers' trials

The drive to transform Soviet industry was accompanied by a revolution in education and the re-establishment of harsh social discipline.

- As part of the offensive to modernise rapidly, technical education was made widely available and was seen as the basis of a cultural revolution.
- In June 1929 all graduate training in technical subjects was made faster as part of the process of creating a new elite.
- At the beginning of 1930, Stalin launched the so called 'socialist offensive' to reach the targets of the Five Year Plan. However, undertaking such an enterprise caused massive upheaval.
- In November and December 1930, a number of industrial experts led by Professor Ramzin – the so-called Industrial Party – were placed on trial for supposed wrecking.
- Simultaneously, the system of the **Gulag** (a network of forced labour camps) was being created deliberately to mobilise labour.
- In February 1931, Stalin made an unintentionally prophetic speech to

Moscow workers in which he attempted to justify the tempo of change. It is important in highlighting the urgency with which industrialisation was undertaken; 'We are 50 to a 100 years behind the advanced countries. We must make good this distance in 10 years or they will crush us.'

- Work discipline was tightened with prison sentences for offences which broke labour discipline being introduced in January 1931. This was followed in February with the introduction of labour books for all factory workers.

Not all the incentives to work hard were negative.
- In June 1931, Stalin reversed the official policy of sanctioning attacks on the 'bourgeois engineers' – their technical skills were too important to industry.
- In the same month he signalled the end of equal wages for all work and introduced differentials between skilled and unskilled labour. This process was part of an overall strategy to build a new elite based on technical education and loyalty to Stalin. By the start of 1932 the Politburo was packed with Stalin supporters such as Ordzhonikidze and Kirov.

## Crisis, 1932–33

The years 1932–33 were extremely hard, with a decline in living standards and a further reinforcement of discipline. Crisis gripped the economy with inflation rising sharply and famine in the country. As conditions worsened in the Soviet Union, there were rumblings of discontent:
- In **August 1932**, M N Ryutin, who was an officer of the Central Committee Secretariat and an influential communist, issued a damning critique of Stalinist policies. He was expelled from the Party with his fellow conspirators but sentenced to only 10 years imprisonment. This highlights the fact that Stalin's grip on power was by no means absolute at this stage.
- The worse the economic and social conditions, the more frequent was the unmasking of conspiracies. In **January 1933** workers from power stations (including six Britons) were charged with sabotage in what became known as the **Metro–Vickers trial**. Although found guilty in April 1933, the Britons were allowed to leave the country soon after.

## Planning for the second Five Year Plan

By December 1932 the first Five Year Plan was officially declared to have been completed and Gosplan laid the plans for the second Five Year Plan which was to run from 1933–37. The targets were less ambitious than those of the first in the light of the poor economic performance in 1933, but followed the same lines (i.e. mechanisation in agriculture, investment in heavy industry and the expansion of education). In fact, the plan adopted by the XVIIth Party Congress in January 1934 was distinctly pragmatic.

## The XVII Party Congress and the murder of Kirov

- So as retain some control of the Party, to embark on a new revolutionary course and to silence internal dissent, there was a purge of nearly one million members (nearly one-third of the total membership) from the start of 1933 until 1935. The whole process of 'disciplining' the party was co-ordinated by Nikolai Yezhov head of the **NKVD**.
- The Congress in 1934 had a far wider significance than simply the adoption of the second Five Year Plan. Because of the significant hardship of the previous years, there was some opposition to Stalin at this supposed 'Congress of Victors'. Behind the overwhelming praise of Stalin was a move to replace him with **Kirov** as General Secretary. In the secret ballot for the Central Committee, almost a quarter of the electorate (270 delegates) voted against Stalin. The dictator bided his time to revenge himself on the old Bolsheviks of the Congress.
- In July 1934 the whole apparatus of repression was reorganised, the NKVD swallowed up the OGPU and thereby gained control of the Gulag empire and secret police. At its head was the ever-loyal Yagoda, with Yezhov taking the leading role in implementing Stalin's instructions.
- The **Great Purges** date from the 1 December 1934 when Kirov was shot dead in the Smolny Institute, Leningrad by a young communist named Leonid Nikolaev. The following day the NKVD was given powers to arrest, try and execute suspects. Thousands were arrested in the wake of the Kirov assassination including leading Bolsheviks, Kamenev and Zinoviev who were placed on trial in January 1935 for Kirov's murder. They were both imprisoned for 5 and 10 years respectively.

## The purging machinery

The purging continued apace as the machinery to do it developed:
- In April 1935 the death penalty was extended to be used on those as young as 12 when appropriate.
- Three months later a form of hostage system was introduced whereby all members of a family could be punished if one of their members was deemed to be disloyal.
- Important communist institutions came under suspicion. **Komsomol** (the youth organisation) was purged and later in 1935, the Society of Old Bolsheviks was disbanded.

## The second Five Year Plan

Preparation for the second Five Year Plan happened against an improving economic background. The time 1934–36 was known as 'three good years', with significant growth in sectors such as the metal industry.

- Investments made from 1928 were now bearing fruit and the second Five Year Plan saw a flourishing of new enterprises, around 4500 in all, as opposed to 1500 from 1928–33.
- There was also a rise in labour productivity which was partly fuelled by the **Stakanovite movement**. **Aleksei Stakhanov** was a miner from the Donbass region who was said to have over fulfilled his production quota by 1400%. Those who also over fulfilled their quotas were given special privileges as 'Stakhanov' workers.
- Although the planned rise in investment in the consumer goods industry did not materialise, this was mainly due to increase in defence spending – in 1933 it accounted for 3.4% of expenditure whereas in 1937 this had risen to 16.5%.
- On the other hand, rationing was phased out in 1935 and money wages nearly doubled between 1933–37, with real wages also rising.
- The drive to educate a new technical elite continued, producing 290,000 engineering graduates between 1928–40.

## A new constitution, 1936

A new constitution was presented to the Soviet Union in June 1936 which promised numerous liberties including freedom of speech, religious belief and assembly, the right to work, equality between the sexes and universal suffrage. Although it even recognised the right of republics to withdraw from the Soviet Union, the constitution was as much a vehicle for institutionalising the role of the Party. Its introduction masked the preparations made for the campaign to denounce and eliminate all those considered to be 'enemies of the people', i.e. enemies of Stalin.

## The Great Purge trials, 1936

- In July 1936 accusations were made against **Kamenev, Zinoviev** and **Ivan Smirnov** that they and others had organised the attack on Kirov and that they were planning to assassinate the rest of the Soviet leadership. In the end, 'confessions' were wrung out of 14 of the supposed 'Trotskyite-Zinovievite Centre' and all 16 defendants at the first show trial were shot in August. This was an important turning point: from now on all 'opposition' was to be treated without mercy.
- The defendants of the next trial included **Radek** and **Piatakov**. The former spent the trial repeating all that the NKVD told him to say, including the repeated and unprompted mentioning of Marshal Tukhachchevsky who was overall Commander of the Red Army. Despite the interventions of his boss, **Ordzhonikidze** who was Commissar of Heavy Industry, Piatakov was indicted on charges of sabotage and wrecking, even though it was he more than any other who had planned the Five Year Plan. He was shot whereas Radek was only imprisoned.

## The Yezhovshchina

The period spanning the years 1936–38 are known as the Yezhovshchina, which literally means the 'years of Yezhov'. Nicolai Yezhov, nicknamed the 'bloody dwarf', was the head of the NKVD (Secret Police) at this time.

- A whirlwind of denunciations, arrests and accusations swept the country completely destabilising all social institutions.
- The turning point was the February–March Central Committee plenum of 1937. At this, not only were Bukharin and Rykov denounced and arrested, but Stalin clearly hinted that the forthcoming purges would be extended to cover the whole Soviet elite.
- In June 1937, **Marshall Tukhachevsky** and eight other leading members of the Red Army High Command were arrested. They were tried and shot almost immediately and their families imprisoned or executed.
- In the events that followed some 43,000 of the most experienced officers were purged including 3 out of 5 marshals, 50 out of 57 corps commanders, 154 out of the 186 divisional commanders and 221 out of 397 brigade commanders.
- The Old Bolsheviks were simultaneously purged. Of the 1966 delegates to the XVIIth Party Congress, 1108 were executed, as were 98 of the 139 members of the CC they elected.

## The Gulag swells

- In Leningrad from May 1937, a vicious assault on the Party hierarchy was unleashed by Zhdanov, partly because of the level of mistrust Stalin held for the city, but also because all NKVD units were given their quotas to fulfil. The Ukrainian Communist Party was obliterated, with only 3 out of 102 members of its Central Committtee surviving, and right across the Soviet Union those who had led the industrialisation process were destroyed.
- By the end of 1937 the Gulag is estimated to have had over 6 million inmates, perhaps as many as 600,000 being former Party members. Figures fluctuate widely for the numbers arrested and killed during the Yezhov years, but it has been suggested that there were up 7 million arrests. Rapid economic growth demanded cheap and expendable labour and the Gulag was the means by which this labour was provided. The numbers involved made it an important part of the Soviet economy.

## The trial of Bukharin, Yagoda and Rykov

In January 1938, Yezhov was replaced by **Beria**, his task completed. The numbers purged began to drop and by 1939 some prisoners were actually released from the Gulag and rehabilitated. This was overshadowed by the Great Purge Trial of **Bukharin, Yagoda, Rykov** and the last remaining Old Bolsheviks held in March 1938.

- The trial was of individuals from many parts of the Soviet establishment, in an attempt to present all the different types of opposition, from Rightists to Trotskyites, as being linked.
- There were a variety of charges ranging from treason to the murder of the writer Maxim Gorky (who died of poisoning in June 1936). Bukharin was even charged with attempting to overthrow Lenin in 1918. All defendants were found guilty and all bar three were shot almost immediately.

## The third Five Year Plan

The XVIIIth Party Congress adopted the third Five Year Plan which was much in tune with the previous plans, i.e. giving precedence to heavy industry with around 5400 new industrial projects being planned. This continuity was reinforced with further measures to tighten discipline. In 1940 a new labour law was introduced which extended the working day by an hour, made a criminal offence of absenteeism (defined as being over 20 minutes late) and abolished the right of labour to switch jobs.

How to Pass AS Modern World History

# Assessment: Soviet industrialisation and the purges

## Questions in the style of OCR (Unit 3)

**Q 1 a Explain how the Soviet Union was transformed under Stalin in the 1930s.** (30)

## How to answer this question

You must make sure that you balance your answer, explaining the significance of the factors you have identified in detail. Here are some examples of factors you might choose:
- the Five Year Plans
- the purges
- education
- collectivisation of agriculture.

Before you start, you should write a plan. The plan should include a main theme for each factor. Here are two examples (although these ideas are quite straightforward, they would allow you to write with confidence).
- Collectivisation was an economic and social revolution which transformed the countryside in the Soviet Union in the 1930s.
- The purges were the means by which Stalin transformed Soviet society and created his own political power.

The extract below focuses on the way in which purging transformed the Soviet Union. In this extract the candidate has explained how the purging altered Soviet politics. In the paragraph after this one, the candidate went on to discuss the effects of the purges on society and the creation of forced labour.

Purging was the means by which politics in the Soviet Union was transformed. Stalin's control was asserted and non-Russian nationalism and potential opposition crushed. In this process Lenin's Bolshevik Party was destroyed. There was opposition within the Communist Party to the scale and the tempo of industrialisation and this became acutely apparent in 1934 at the XVIIth Party Congress. Of the 1966 members of the XVIIth Party Congress, 1108 were executed in the following years. The assassination of Kirov in 1934 marked the beginnings of a complete political transformation. The Party and its leading members were in the way of the personal dictatorship which Stalin believed was essential for economic change. Therefore, between 1934–38 the core members of Lenin's Party, including Bukharin, Rykov and Kamenev, were executed after show trials. A new leadership loyal to Stalin emerged including Khrushchev and Molotov. They helped Stalin destroy any independence in the non-Russian parts of the Soviet Union, e.g. in the late 1930s, 99 out of 102 members of the Ukrainian Communist Party were purged.

Q **b Compare the importance of at least three of the factors you have looked at in your answer to 1a in bringing about change in the Soviet Union in the 1930s.** **(60)**

## How to answer this question

The question is asking you to weigh up the relative importance of the different factors. You need to back up your analysis with sufficient evidence. The key to a clear response in these questions is effective planning – your lines of argument must be clear before you write. Here are examples of the key arguments you might put into an introduction.

- The most important factor in bringing about a transformation of the Soviet Union was industrialisation. The pace of industrialisation and the need for resources was an important reason for the social and political changes which took place in the 1930s.
- However, purging was the tool with which Stalin ensured economic change would take place.
- Collectivisation ensured communist control of the countryside and of agricultural resources, so important if economic change was to take place.

## Further question in the style of OCR (Unit 3)

Q **2 a Examine the effects of the first Five Year Plan on Soviet society and the economy.** **(30)**
**b Why were so many Soviet citizens purged in the 1930s?** **(60)**

# Section 6: The Soviet Union, the Second World War and the Cold War

## Pact with Nazi Germany

- The outbreak of the Second World War in 1939 saw the Soviet Union maintain her neutrality as a consequence of the **Molotov–Rippentrop Pact** signed on 23 August 1939.
- Almost immediately on 28 September, Germany and the Soviet Union agreed to partition Poland, placing 13 million Poles under direct Stalinist rule.
- The Baltic States similarly fell into the new Soviet sphere of influence from late 1939. The consequence was that nearly 700,000 Lithuanians were sent eastwards, as were up to 1.25 million Poles.

## Invasion and the relocation of industry

On 22 June 1941, the Nazis unleashed **Operation Barbarossa**, their military campaign to defeat the Soviet Union and destroy communism.

- The aim was a **Blitzkreig** (bombing) campaign which would see the rapid defeat of the Red Army and the occupation of the Caucuses with its rich oil fields. The start of the campaign caught the Soviets off-guard and by the end of July, considerable progress had been made. However, the primary objectives of Moscow, Leningrad and the Donets Basin had not yet been reached.
- On 4 September, Leningrad was besieged and by the end of October the Germans had laid siege to Moscow from the north. The Soviets counterattacked on 6 December and pushed the German forces back. The German attempt to defeat the Soviet Union in one campaign had failed, in part because of the delays and the weather, but also because the size of such an operation was beyond the means of the Wehrmacht.

## The effect on industry

- So deep had the Wehrmacht penetrated by the end of 1941 that the civilian economy lay in tatters. To deny the invader any sustenance, Stalin ordered a 'scorched earth policy' – everything was to be destroyed. Important areas such as the coal and iron-producing Donbass region were lost to the Germans early on. In all, some 45% of the Soviet Union's industrial capacity was lost to the invader.
- Despite the loss of industrial capacity as a result of the invasion, whole factories were dismantled and moved 1500 miles or so eastwards to the Urals, Central Asia and Siberia. There they were reconstructed and began to produce for the war effort.
- By the end of 1941, 1523 factories had been reconstructed in the East. Some factories such as the **Kirov tank factory** in Leningrad moved almost immediately in June 1941. By New Year 1943 the Soviet Union

was out producing the German economy in terms of quantity and quality of munitions. During the war, Soviet industry produced over 95,000 tanks and 108,000 planes. Such an effort was the cause of the eventual defeat of the Nazis.

## Stalingrad

- Buoyed by the success of the defence of Moscow, Stalin ordered a winter counter-offensive, pushing the lines of the invaders back over 300 miles in places. The Wehrmacht suffered some 400,000 casualties before the attack ended in April.
- In May 1942, the German troops attempted to drive through the Crimea and on to the oil fields of the Caucuses. Initially the campaign was successful – in June they captured the Crimea and Sevastopol.
- The Army in the South continued to advance and in August it crossed the Don River and opened the attack on the strategically important city of Stalingrad.
- Beyond Stalingrad, Hitler had already sent the Fourth Panzer Army into the Caucuses. This was a crucial error. Having divided his forces, Hitler failed to take account of what was needed to take Stalingrad, or the growing resistance of its defenders.
- In September the Germans penetrated the city but could not take it.
- In late November, the Red Army succeeded in encircling the Sixth Army in a pincer movement. Despite Hitler's insistence that there would be no surrender, the depleted Germans surrendered at Stalingrad on 2 February 1943. The battle had cost the lives of nearly 2 million men (some 1.1 million Soviets and 800,000 Axis soldiers). It proved to be the decisive turning point of the war.
- Having been turned at Stalingrad, the Wehrmacht was pushed ever further back. Soviet industrial superiority was underlined by the victory of its tanks at the monumental battle of Kursk in July 1943. Then followed what became known as Stalin's Ten Great Battles, which propelled the Red Army to the gates of Berlin and victory in May 1945.

## The countryside and the Second World War

The war placed further massive burdens on the countryside, with industry and military operations taking precedence.

- Vast areas of the countryside were overrun and subjugated by the Nazis, including the fertile lands of the Ukraine.
- There was massive depopulation, some 60% of the Soviet Army being from the countryside and no agricultural occupation being treated as a 'reserved profession'. In fact, the agricultural workforce was reduced by anything up to 19 million people between 1941–44.
- In tandem with this was a de-mechanisation which also resulted in a fall

How to Pass AS Modern World History

in production. The MTSs (Machine Tractor Stations) were starved of technicians and machines, all tractor factories temporarily producing tanks until 1944.

- In 1943 agricultural output was at only 38% of its 1940 level. This provoked the regime into squeezing the agricultural sector even more tightly with the help of political commissars sent in to run the kolkhozes in November 1941.
- The peasantry were forced to work harder by even more draconian regulations. In April 1942 the minimum work expected from each peasant was increased and failure to fulfil one's daily labour quota rendered an individual liable to punishment.
- During wartime, the state requisitioned practically all produce from the countryside but it turned a blind eye to the black market. The war had seen some loosening of state control, in 1942 the army had been given a degree of independence and political commissars abolished. It was not until the end of the war that the Party reasserted a level of control.

## The fourth Five Year Plan

The post-war years saw a re-establishment of the repressive Stalinist regime and the planned economy.

- There is no doubt of the devastating effect of the war on industry as a whole, not least the loss of 27 million lives. By 1945, 51% of workers in industry were women, nearly 4.8 million of them. Over 65,000 km of track had been destroyed during the war and some 3.5 million homes.
- The fourth Five Year Plan was introduced in 1945 with the aim of restoring heavy industry to its pre-war levels and to an extent it achieved those aims, e.g. electricity output was higher in 1950 than 10 years earlier.

## The re-introduction of purging

Although this re-industrialisation was not accompanied by the same level of political violence, purging was again used as a means of centralisation and control.

- 1946–48 was a period of so-called 'party renewal' – termed the **Zhdanovshchina** ('in the time of Zhdanov').
- During the war Zhdanov ran the Leningrad Defence Council, and the first act of 'ideological regeneration' in August 1946 was an attack on two literary journals from that city, *Zvezda* and *Leningrad*.
- This was followed by the widespread denunciation and humiliation of those who had supposedly strayed from the conformity of 'socialist realism'. Those who were expelled from Writers and Composers Unions included the great filmmakers Eisenstein and Pudovkin.
- In February 1948 the composers Shostakovich and Prokofiev were attacked for writing elitist and 'non-Russian' music.

## Russification and anti-Semitism post 1945

As the war was defined as 'the Great Patriotic War', those nations within the Empire which were considered to be anti-Russian were attacked.

- Ukrainian nationalism was suppressed and Soviet Jews came under attack, particularly after the declaration of an independent Israel in 1948.
- A leading Jewish actor, Solomon Mikhoels died in suspicious circumstances in 1948, the same year that the Jewish Anti-Fascist Committee was closed down.
- In the last years of Stalin's life, the Jewish people suffered considerable persecution. By 1952, there were quotas for Jews in most universities, Jewish schools had been shut and Jewish employment in State organisations was limited.
- This anti-Semitism peaked in August 1952 with the arrest and execution of Solomon Losovsky (who was an ex-Deputy Foreign Minister), and 12 leading Jewish writers and scholars.
- In the bizarre '**Doctors Case**' of 1952–53, nine doctors were named as having conspired to kill Stalin and having murdered Zhdanov.

## The aftermath of war

Despite the huge sacrifices of the agricultural sector during the war, the resumption of peace saw a return to the strict regulation by central authority of the pre-war years:

- In September 1946 the State passed a decree demanding the return to the kolkhoz of all land the system had previously owned.
- The burden of taxation was again placed on the kolkhozes and procurement levels of grain and livestock were increased by 50%.
- In 1950, a drive to amalgamate smaller kolkhozes into larger ones was undertaken by **Nikita Khrushchev** and a proposal made to set up large agro-towns. The former proposals resulted in a decline in the number of kolkhozes, the latter came to nothing.
- Until the death of Stalin in 1953, there were no measures introduced which improved the life of the kolkhoznik. State prices paid for goods in 1952 were lower than in 1940 and greater taxes on the private plot led to a decline in output.

## Russia and the Cold War, 1945

The wartime alliance with the USA and Britain began to crumble as the end of the war approached. Stalin's aims at the end of the war were as follows:

- to create a Soviet sphere of influence in eastern Europe which would act as a buffer zone against the capitalist west
- to collect reparations – the economic devastation caused by the loss

during the war of around 27 million people meant that Stalin sought reparations from conquered territory

- to protect the Soviet Union and satellite communist states from what Stalin believed would be inevitable capitalist aggression.

## Yalta and Poland

At the heart of the initial disagreements between Stalin and the Soviet Union's allies was the post-war settlement of eastern Europe.

- In January 1945 the Soviets announced that they had conquered the whole of Poland.
- At the meeting of the wartime allies at **Yalta** in February 1945 it was agreed that the Polish borders were to be altered, with the USSR gaining substantial territories in the east.
- The communist-dominated Lublin government was to be expanded to include members of the Polish government in exile, and free elections were to be held as soon as possible. It was over the definition of 'free elections' that the allies disagreed. To Stalin, opposition to communism was not to be tolerated in what were to become the Soviet satellite States.
- At the **Potsdam Conference** in July and August 1945 tension over the issue of Polish elections re-emerged but was unresolved. The Americans also chose Potsdam to announce to the Soviets the existence of the atomic bomb.

## Soviet control of eastern Europe

In the Soviet-occupied countries of eastern Europe, the Russians used similar tactics to bring the countries under political control.

- In most countries the Soviets set up anti-Fascist coalition governments which were dominated by the communists.
- In Poland the Government of National Unity, led by communist **Osobka–Morawski**, was set up in June 1945.
- In Romania a government led by communist **Petru Groza** was created in March of the same year. Elections were then held which were rigged and in which opposition parties were intimidated.
- In Bulgaria, Czechoslovakia and Romania in 1946, and in Poland and Hungary in 1947, elections produced victory for the communists.
- All states then imposed Stalinist systems of government, opposition was repressed, land nationalised and a centrally planned economy created.
- In Czechoslovakia the communists, led by **Klement Gottwald**, murdered the Foreign Minister Jan Masaryk in March 1948 before setting up forced labour camps in the same year.
- In January 1949 the Soviet Union and its eastern European satellite states set up the **Council for Mutual Economic Assistance** in response to the Marshall Aid programme.

- In September 1949 the Soviets exploded their first atomic bomb.
- The emergence of communist China in 1949 and the start of the Korean War in 1950 reflected the high level of tension between the two blocks.

## Berlin and Germany

Much of the Cold War tension revolved around the issue of Germany and Berlin.

- In 1945 the defeated Germany was divided into four zones, each dominated by one of the four victorious allies.
- In the Soviet zone Stalin ordered far reaching land reforms by the end of 1945.
- The politics of the eastern part of Germany were dominated by the communist Social Unity Party, founded in 1946. However, it became increasingly clear to Stalin that the western allies wished to exclude Soviet influence from the western sector of Berlin and Germany as a whole.
- In December 1946 Britain and the United States merged their zones into one economic zone with the aim of stimulating economic regeneration (Bizonia).
- In June 1947 a German Economic Council was created to direct economic reconstruction.
- Throughout the year Stalin became increasingly frustrated with the western powers' refusal to accept that $10 billion worth of reparations should be paid out of German industrial production.
- In 1948 Stalin ordered the Soviet delegation to walk out of the **Allied Control Council** which ruled Berlin in an attempt to prevent the creation of a separate West German State.
- However, in June 1948 a draft constitution was drawn up from West Germany and the western powers announced the creation of a new German currency, the **Deutschemark**. This new currency was to be used in the non-Soviet sectors including West Berlin.

## The Berlin Airlift and aftermath

- In an attempt to prevent such political and financial reform, Stalin ordered the blockade of Berlin, which continued from July 1948 until May 1949.
- In that time Berlin was provisioned by 277,264 allied flights in what became known as the Berlin Airlift.
- The blockade failed, as did attempts by the Soviets to pressurise western Berlin into political union with the eastern sector.
- In November 1948 the Soviet-backed Berlin Municipal Assembly set up a new administration, claiming authority over the whole of Berlin. In the western sector this move was ignored.
- In October 1949 the **German Democratic Republic** (GDR) was

established in the Soviet sector of East Germany and the Soviet Military Government was replaced by a Soviet Control Commission, which effectively made East Germany another Soviet satellite State.

- Stalin continued to feel threatened by a strong capitalist West German State and the American-dominated anti-Soviet **North Atlantic Treaty Organisation** (NATO), created in 1949.

# Assessment: the Soviet Union, the Second World War and the Cold War

## Question in the style of OCR (Unit 3)

**Q 1 a Explain how external factors influenced Soviet foreign policy in the period 1941–53.** (30)

### How to answer this question

In this question you are being asked to show an understanding of the main influences on Soviet foreign policy in the period stated. In your answer you should link the factors you have chosen and the impact they had on Soviet foreign policy. Here are some of the factors you might choose:
• Operation Barbarossa
• Yalta and Potsdam
• the status of Germany, 1945–49
• the nuclear threat.

In your plan you should identify the key themes and then list the ways in which the factors you have explained had an impact. Here is a plan for an answer which discusses the impact of the status of Germany as a significant factor.
• Germany became the focal point of Cold War aggression. Events there between 1945–49 convinced Stalin of the need to create a distinct East Germany and to end co-operation with the Soviet Union's wartime allies.
• Points to include are the introduction of Bizonia and the Deutschemark, the Berlin Blockade, and the creation of the GDR.
• Also cover the attitude of western allies towards reparations, e.g. at Moscow Conference 1947, leading the Soviets to set up a separate economic zone in the East.

**Q b Compare the importance of at least three factors in influencing Soviet foreign policy.** (60)

### How to answer this question

You need to look at the relative importance of the factors you have chosen, the links between them and provide a comparison, placing them in order of importance. It is essential that you make your links as explicit as possible. In your plan you should identify your main points of argument and then briefly list what you will discuss in each paragraph. Here is an example of some key points you might make.
• Operation Barbarossa had the most profound impact on Soviet foreign

policy. It brought the Soviet Union into alliance with Britain, and eventually the USA, against Nazi Germany. It also marked the beginning of war which was to lead to Soviet occupation of eastern Europe.

- Yalta and Potsdam marked a turning point of Soviet foreign policy away from the alliance and into the Cold War. This was very much linked to the nuclear issue which increased tensions between the two sides.

Here is an extract from an answer to this question. In the extract there are attempts to link explicitly the factors.

> Soviet foreign policy was very much affected by the Potsdam Conference. The crucial factors at Potsdam were the attitude of Truman towards the Soviet Union and the announcement that the Americans had the bomb. Although Stalin had information about the nuclear project, it was Truman's aggressive stance about Polish elections and rejection of Soviet influence in western Europe which convinced Stalin of the need to reinforce Soviet dominance of eastern Europe.

## Further questions in the style of OCR (Unit 3)

Q 2 a **Explain the effects of the Second World War by 1945 on the USSR.** (30)

b **Why did Stalinism change so little in the years 1945-53?** (60)

Q 3 a **Explain why the alliance against the Nazis collapsed in the period 1945–49.** (30)

b **Using what means and how successfully did the Soviet Union extend its control over eastern Europe in the period 1945-53?** (60)

# Chapter 4
## Italy, 1914–45

## Section 1: War and the rise of fascism, 1914–25

### Introduction

From 1871 to the eve of the First World War, the Liberal State in Italy was dominated by a narrow political establishment. This maintained power by absorbing elements of different political groups into its structure, thereby gaining acceptance from their supporters. This system was undermined by the emergence of mass politics and the consequences of the First World War.

### To fight or not to fight?

Growing social unrest was overshadowed by the rush to war which followed the assassination of Archduke Franz Ferdinand in Sarajevo on 28 June 1914. The Italian foreign minister **Antonio di San Giuliano** and his successor **Sidney Sonnino** were faced with the dilemma of whether Italy should stay neutral or intervene in the war. If the latter course was chosen, there was the further dilemma of which side Italy should join.

- **Fight against Germany and Austria-Hungary?** By the terms of the **Triple Alliance**, Italy was bound to stay neutral if an ally, i.e. Austria, or Germany, declared war on another country. Italy had been a founder member of the Triple Alliance in 1882. It was signed as a defensive, conservative alliance and it formed the basis of Italian foreign policy until 1914. Italian military planning still relied on fighting on the side of Austria-Hungary and Germany. However for many Italians, Italy's main enemy was the Austrian Empire which held territory they coveted, such as Trent and Trieste. Many Italians feared that an Austrian victory would lead her to extend her influence in the Balkans and leave Italy without the land she desired.

- **War against the entente powers?** War against Britain would threaten Italy's supply of coal and other raw materials, whilst leaving her coastline exposed to the British Royal Navy. However, the Chief of Staff, **General Cadorna**, calculated that victory against France would be swift and might bring Nice, Corsica and Tunisia into Italian hands. To the more conservative politicians, war against republican France was ideologically the preferable option.

### Entry into war

The decision to enter the war in March 1915 was taken by politicians Salandra and Sonnino. Their guiding principle was that of '**sacro egoismo**'.

In practice, this meant that all decisions would be made on the basis of their potential benefits for Italy. Consequently, Italy signed the **Treaty of London** with Britain and France in April 1915.

- Italy was promised Trieste, Dalmatia, Trentino, the South Tyrol and Istria. These territories would be given to Italy when the war was won, and this was conditional on a declaration of war against Austria. War was declared against Italy's former ally in May 1915.
- The treaty was signed without the knowledge of the army, Parliament or the political nation. The King, **Victor Emmanuel III**, authorised the treaty despite the news of an Arab uprising in Libya which had chased the Italian army across the desert.
- The actions of the King and his ministers sparked off the so-called **'interventionist crisis'**. Led by Giolitti, many deputies showed support for a continuation of the state of neutrality. The political turmoil of May 1915 had important repercussions. Giolitti's opposition to the war meant that support for the war could be portrayed as support for war against the Austrian Empire, and against the system and parliamentary order which Giolitti symbolised.

## The military war 1915–18

The Italian army entered the First World War completely unprepared for the type of warfare which it was to face.

- It lacked the necessary technology and training to fight trench warfare, having only 300 working machine guns.
- Throughout the war, the Army suffered from poor morale and poor leadership. The 5 million conscript troops were mainly southerners. They were paid only half a lira a day and were poorly nourished. The Italians made the mistake of reducing the bread ration in December 1916.
- Discipline in the Army was excessive with over 6% of the ranks being tried by Court Marshal, mostly for desertion.
- Despite the capture of Gorizia in the summer of 1916, military successes were few and far between. The defeat at **Caporetto** in October 1917 was a national humiliation. Most of Veneto was lost and 300,000 men were taken prisoner. This battle was a crushing defeat for the Italian Army and a severe blow to national prestige.
- General Cadorna was replaced by General Diaz who was a more cautious military strategist. In the last days of the war with the Austrian Empire crumbling, Italian troops overran Trieste, Trent and Veneto.

## Political divisions

Throughout the war there was no pro-war majority in the Chamber of Deputies.

- From May 1915 to June 1916, Salandra's government relied on conservative support and that of more democratic **'interventionists'**, such as Nitti. This was the label given to those who supported the war. There were different types of 'interventionists' – some wanted a war for territorial gain; others hoped that war would lead to changes in the Italian constitution.

- The interventionists formed themselves into the 'Parliamentary Group of National Defence' to counterbalance the opponents of war.
- The problem for the government was that it was effectively sidelined by General Cadorna – the Chief of Staff who exercised his influence in the name of the King.
- Therefore, the government had little influence in the running of the war, e.g. the dismissal of Salandra's idea in January 1916 for a more effective war council to co-ordinate the military campaigns.
- In June 1916 Salandra's Cabinet resigned to be led by the ineffective Boselli. His government in turn made way in October 1917 for one led by Orlando in the wake of defeat at Caporetto.

## Opponents

There were many opponents of the war in Italy.
- Those who identified with Giolitti, formed themselves into the **'Parliamentary Union'** in 1917.
- In August 1915, Pope Benedict XV called the war 'appalling butchery'.
- His sentiments were shared by rioting crowds in Turin in September in the same month.
- On the left, there was widespread support for **neutralism** as shown by the socialist PSI's (Partito Socialista Italiano) leadership, the Directorate, and its popular paper *Avanti*. However, many socialist deputies such as Bissolati were drawn into the 'democratic interventionist' camp on the grounds of patriotic duty.

The war polarised the socialist movement as it divided the political nation. This was made worse by the publication in 1918 of the **Treaty of London** by the Bolshevik government in Russia, which showed that the Italians were fighting for land outside their proposed national borders, i.e. northern Dalmatia and the South Tyrol. This offended many 'democratic interventionists' such as the Republican Leonida Barzilia, who called for a revision of war aims to leave out such territorial claims. This brought them into conflict with more conservative interventionists and nationalists who pressed for the extension of borders. By the armistice of 1918, the political nation was more deeply divided than at any time previously.

## The economic war

The economic policy followed by the state from 1915–18 was growth at any cost.
- Production of munitions rose spectacularly. By 1918, 6500 planes were

being produced per year and **Fiat** was making over 24,000 lorries, as opposed to just over 4,000 in 1914.

- The state was plunged heavily into debt as a result of the war, the national debt rising from 15.7 billion lire in 1914 to 84.9 billion lire in 1918.
- Even more threatening to social stability was that prices rose steeply in the same period, which led to a decline in real wages of about 25% and frustration was compounded by a long working week and poor living conditions. In August 1917, serious riots broke out in Turin.
- Inflation also changed attitudes in the countryside, many peasants taking advantage of rising prices and fixed rents to pay off their debts. This led to an increased demand for land ownership, a fact recognised in the government propaganda of 1918 which promised 'land for the peasants'. In the same year there were examples of peasant land occupation in Emilia to the north of Italy and around Rome.

## Versailles

The fact that the war had ended victoriously, coupled with the uncompromising behaviour of Orlando and Sonnino at the peace talks at Versailles, raised popular expectations of significant territorial gains. Not only did the two politicians press for the terms of the Treaty of London to be implemented in full but, at Sonnino's insistence, the Italian delegation demanded the port of **Fiume** and the whole of **Dalmatia** (the Treaty of London had promised half of Dalmatia). In the end, Italy received the sizeable territories of **Trent, Trieste, Aldo Adige and Istria**, yet the myth that Italy had won only a '**mutilated victory**' was already widespread because she was denied Fiume, Dalmatia and any of Germany's colonial possessions. The consequence was unrest amongst 'interventionist' groups who felt that Italy had been betrayed. The term 'mutilated victory' was coined by nationalist **Gabriele d'Annunzio**. It meant that, although Italy had been on the winning side in the war, her victory was lessened.

## Proportional representation

In May 1919, Orlando's government was replaced by one led by Francesco Nitti. This government introduced proportional representation, on the surface to reward the soldiers, but in the main to destroy the basis of Giolitti's political system (since proportional representation would result in the election of deputies from the socialist and Catholic-backed parties, and deputies from these parties were not likely to be manipulated by Giolitti). Nitti's government was completely undermined by the actions of the nationalist writer and leader, Gabriele D'Annunzio.

- In September 1919, D'Annunzio marched into Fiume with 2,000 supporters, and declared the town annexed to Italy. This was done with the knowledge of the Italian army. Not only were his actions extremely popular, they legitimised extra-parliamentary action and, for 15 months, stood as a symbol of the inadequacies of parliamentary government.

- The **Treaty of Rapallo** of November 1920 between Italy and Yugoslavia declared Fiume independent, thereby satisfying many nationalists who were simply interested in keeping it out of Yugoslavian hands. In December 1920, Giolitti sent the Italian navy to Fiume and D'Annunzio surrendered. This was a decisive step on the part of Giolitti, but otherwise his government and the whole political system was in growing crisis.

## Crisis in the political system

In 1919, the Catholics formed their own political party, the **Partido Popolare Italiano** (PPI).

- The consequence of this was that the liberal politicians could no longer rely on the conservative Catholic vote as they did in 1913 with the Gentiloni Pact.
- In Parliament, however, they came to rely increasingly on the PPI's support – the Party winning 100 seats in the November 1919 election and 107 in May 1921 (in both occasions with around 20% of the vote).
- The new system of proportional representation strengthened the influence of the socialist movement (PSI) – in the same elections they won 156 and 123 seats respectively.

## Economic unrest

Outside Parliament there was increasing industrial militancy, due to inflation and the end of the war – the labour movement being suppressed by wartime measures.

- In 1919, over one million went on strike.
- In April 1920 there was a 10-day General Strike in Piedmont.
- Most significant, was the '**Occupation of the Factories**' of September 1920. What began as a wage strike in the engineering industry developed into the occupation of their factories by 400,000 workers. The government intervened, and promised greater worker participation in the management of industry. As a result, the occupation ended, but not without great bitterness on both sides.

The story was the same in the countryside, with growing numbers of **land occupations** and incidents of violence. The government intervened, yet it seemed to the landowners that it was automatically siding with the peasantry, an example being the decree of October 1920, which granted permanent tenure to illegal occupiers of uncultivated land.

The liberal establishment found it increasingly difficult to form governments against such a backdrop of parliamentary opposition and political instability. Both the governments of **Ivanoe Bonomi** (June 1921 to February 1922) and **Luigi Facta** (February to July 1922, and July to October 1922) failed to stem the growing crisis.

## The rise of fascism

In October 1921, the **Partido Nazionale Fascista** (PNF) was founded by **Benito Mussolini**.

- The party grew quickly and by May 1922 it had 300,000 members.
- The movement had its base in the '**squadrismo**' or squads which comprised its paramilitary section. These were the organised gangs of the fascist movement. Their membership consisted of ex-soldiers. Their tactics were brutal in the extreme. Increasingly used by landowners and the local establishment as the main weapon of law and order and the most effective bulwark against socialism, the squads flourished.
- In 1921, they swept the 'red' provinces of Emelia and Tuscany, breaking strikes and the socialist peasant leagues.

In July and August 1922, fascist volunteers helped ensure the failure of the '**Alliance of Labour**' strike. The strike was backed by the main socialist parties and consisted of some of the most important trade unions, including dockers and railwaymen. Its failure, therefore, was a significant blow to the prestige and power of the socialist movement as a whole.

From then onwards, the fascists held the upper hand and in October 1922, Mussolini pressed for a place in government, backed by the threat of a mobilisation of the fascist militia. The Facta government requested that the King introduce a state of martial law, but on 27 October, Victor Emmanuel III refused to sign the relevant decree, ostensibly to prevent bloodshed. Despite having only 6% of the Chamber's deputies, Mussolini was invited to be Prime Minister on 29 October. The following few days of celebration by the fascist blackshirts were later transformed into the myth of the '**March on Rome**'.

## The Fascist consolidation of power

- In his first so-called 'National Government', Mussolini included representatives of the PPI and liberal establishment (there were four liberal ministers and three from the PPI in the government).
- In January 1923, the squads were tamed by the creation of a new organisation, the **Fascist Militia** (MVSN) which was placed under the centralised control of Mussolini.
- To remove the problems of PSI and PPI representation, the electoral law was revised in 1923 to a system whereby the party with the largest number of votes (as long as it achieved over 25%), received two-thirds of the parliamentary seats.

- In April 1924, the right-wing 'list' of candidates received 66.3% of the votes anyway, approximately 60% of this coalition being fascists.

## The murder of Matteotti

The most outspoken critic of increasing fascist domination was the leader of the PSI, **Giacomo Matteotti**.

- On 11 June 1924 he disappeared, murdered by fascists. Although there was no direct evidence linking the fascists to the murder, Matteotti's defiant speech against the rigging of the 1924 election made him an obvious target for the squads.
- In the furore following the assassination, the PSI walked out of the Chamber of Deputies and Mussolini's government was plunged into crisis. The opposition hesitated, however, and Mussolini was able to seize the political initiative.
- On the 3 January 1925, he reassured the establishment that he would reassert law and order and restore strong government. The Matteotti crisis was a watershed and it was the last chance to remove Mussolini from the centre of power for, it transpired, nearly 20 years, but a chance which was missed.

# Assessment: War and the rise of fascism, 1914–25

**Questions in the style of Edexcel (Unit 2)**

**Q 1a  Explain why Mussolini became Prime Minister in 1922.**

(15)

### How to answer this question

This is a straightforward analytical question asking you to consider the reasons for Mussolini's appointment in 1922. The question allows you to open up your analysis to a range of factors. Factors you are likely to include are: the King's actions; support for Mussolini in the army; the failure of the Liberal State in 1922; economic and social unrest, e.g. the Alliance of Labour strike; the violence of the squadristi and the 'March on Rome'.

**Q  b  Describe how Mussolini consolidated power in Italy, 1922–25.**

(15)

### How to answer this question

The question is giving you the opportunity to show that you have a very clear understanding of the way in which Mussolini and the fascists strengthened their grip on power. There are key turning points which you should explain. These include a conservative economic policy, reform of the electoral law, the defeat of the radical fascists and the taming of the squads, the Matteotti crisis and its aftermath, the actions of the King and foreign policy including Corfu (see Unit 3).

When answering these descriptive questions, you must be as clear as possible about the significance of the information you are giving. Look at the example given below and note that the candidate's answer is well structured and uses well-selected evidence. It gives a very clear explanation of the importance of the King in the consolidation of power.

> The actions of the King played an important part in the fascists' consolidation of power. This was most important during the Matteotti crisis. The outcry at the murder of the reformist socialist in June 1924 might well have led to Mussolini's resignation. However, from the start of the crisis, the King backed Mussolini and in July 1924 a royal decree introduced far stricter censorship laws. In July 1924, Bonomi, Sforza and other ex-cabinet ministers gave the King detailed evidence of Mussolini's part in the murder of Matteotti. The King ignored their advice. Even in November and December 1924, when established politicians such as Orlando and senior members of the royal household such as Senator di

Campello began to move against Mussolini, the King consistently refused to dismiss his Prime Minister. Victor Emmanuel also refused to use the army against the fascists, despite growing violence throughout the country by the turn of 1925. The attitude of the King was crucial in explaining the survival of the fascist regime.

## Course essay in the style of AQA (Unit 3)

**Q 2 Explain the reasons why Italy joined the First World War in 1915.**

### How to answer this question

Because this is a course essay question you will have some time to read around the topic and prepare your answer. You should try and make detailed notes on the following:
- relations with Germany
- relations with Austria-Hungary
- how foreign policy decisions were made in Italy
- Sacro egoismo
- reasons for neutrality in 1914
- arguments for and against fighting on the side of Britain and France.

You should plan your answer with a clear line of argument. Here are examples of the type of points you might put into your plan:
- the most important reason why Italy joined the war was the desire to gain territory at the expense of Austria-Hungary
- although there was support amongst the military for fighting against Britain and France there were many reasons why this was not sensible.

## Questions in the style of Edexcel (Unit 2)

**Q 3a Describe the weakness of the Liberal State in the period 1918–22.** (15)

**b Why did King Victor Emmanuel III ask Mussolini to be Prime Minister in 1922?** (15)

**Q 4a Describe the consolidation of fascist power, 1922-25.** (15)

**b Why did support for the fascists increase in the period 1919-22?** (15)

## Course essay in the style of AQA

**Q 5 How important were perceptions of the Treaty of Versailles in explaining D'Annunzio's occupation of Fiume?**

# Section 2: Italy, 1925–40

## Consolidation of power, 1925–28

The period from 1925–28 saw the foundations laid of the new fascist state:

- A series of statutes were passed by the Monarch with little discussion in the Chamber of Deputies.
- Through this legislation of 1925 – the **Legge Fascistissime** – the work of repression was extended. The control over the press was tightened. All journalists were to be registered and every newspaper was to have a director appointed by the government.
- All freemasonry and similar secret society activities were banned in May of that year.
- The next move was to strengthen central government control of local government. Traditionally, the localities were administered by Prefects who were picked from the ranks of career civil servants. Under the fascists their powers were increased, as in 1926 all local councils were disbanded. Their place was taken by the **Podesta** who was appointed by the Prefect. Often they were chosen from the old ruling class.

## Censorship

- In December 1925 a further Press Law was introduced which brought the press even more into line with the regime. Only state-registered journalists could write and their registration could be removed for criticism of the regime.
- Another law of the same month stated that no law could be presented to Parliament without Mussolini's consent and that Cabinet ministers would be responsible to him and not to Parliament. The Monarch's powers were reduced and consisted chiefly of the power to appoint and dismiss the Prime Minister.

## Further repressive measures

- 1926 saw a further increase in repressive legislation.
- In January 1926 the Prime Minister was authorised to **govern by decree** when he believed necessary. This was to form the basis of fascist rule, with over 100,000 laws passed by 1943.
- After three assassination attempts on his life, a law was passed in November 1926 which provided the death penalty for any actions undertaken against the King or the Head of State, i.e. Mussolini.
- In the same month, a '**Special Tribunal for the Defence of the State**' was set up to try opponents of the regime, the so-called 'political trials'.
- All opposition parties were banned and the police were allowed to banish 'enemies of the State' to remote parts of the land (this punishment was known as **confino**). Despite its fearsome name, however, the tribunal passed nine death penalties up until 1940.

## New electoral law

Those deputies who had walked out of the Chamber of Deputies (the lower House of Parliament) in June 1925 in disgust, were barred entry on return. A new electoral law of May 1928 ended any charade of democracy by abolishing universal suffrage and restricting the vote to men aged over 21 who paid syndicate rates or taxes of over 100 lire per annum. In any election the 400 candidates were to be submitted to the electorate by the Fascist Grand Council and voted for or rejected en bloc.

## Fascism restrained, 1926–28

- Whilst altering the institutions of state, Mussolini simultaneously dealt with the more radical elements of the fascist movement itself. In October 1925 he ordered the squadristi to be dissolved and dismissed the powerful PNF Secretary, Roberto Farinacci.
- In 1926 the Party's nature was altered by an influx of new members, 338,000 in one year. These new members were mainly career-minded professionals who recognised that Party membership was going to be essential for career advancement.
- The local structure of the Fascist Party was abolished in October 1926 and the PNF (Partito Nazionale Fascista) reorganised. All appointments were made from above and the Party's political role was ended.
- In February 1928 the Fascist militia was incorporated into the regular army to stop it acting independently. The Fascist Grand Council was made an important organ of state, in theory at least, and given widespread constitutional powers. It became a more important body than either Parliament or the Cabinet. After 1926 it had a say on all constitutional matters, could be consulted on treaties and even could decide on the Crown's powers.

## The corporate state

The economy was to be organised along the lines of a corporate state:
- This meant creating institutions and structures which would incorporate the interests of both employers and workers, who would work together happily in the national interest.
- The strengthening of fascist unions or **syndicates** was a main aim of the new regime. However, it was important that this was at the expense of other non-fascist trade unions and not the business interests which had been so influential in bringing Mussolini to power.
- In April 1926, a law introduced by Alfredo Rocco, the Minister of Justice, recognised a number of syndicates and established compulsory arbitration in industrial disputes. The syndicates were not given a role in government, however, and were forbidden to become involved in strikes or lockouts.
- As part of the 'corporatist' ideology, a **Ministry of Corporations** was set

How to Pass AS Modern World History

up in 1926 to be followed in 1929 by a National Council of Corporations. This latter body was created to arbitrate in disputes in the interests of national production.

### Quota Novanta

Before 1926, Italy had experienced an export-led boom. In 1926 the regime introduced a new exchange rate, the *quota novanta*:

- This move was a very important turning point in economic policy as it marked the start of the long road towards self-sufficiency and an economic policy dominated by fascist gestures.
- The revaluation of the lire from 150 to 90 to the pound encouraged the turn away from exports to an economy dominated by subsidised heavy industry. From this time on, heavy industry prospered under such patronage and protection – steel and chemicals in particular.
- However, not all industry flourished under the *quota novanta* – both the car and textile industries had to diversify to survive.
- To counter the impact of the world-wide depression of the early 1930s, the government lowered money wages and, in November 1934, encouraged a 40-hour working week. This kept unemployment down to perhaps 2.0 million in 1933 and 900,000 in 1936, but at the cost of a reduction in real wages of 10%.

## State-directed capital investment

An important innovation in capital finance took place in 1931 with the creation of the state-backed **industrial finance organisation** (IMI) and in 1933, the **Institute for Industrial Reconstruction** (IRI) which gave industry long-term protection from bankruptcy. The latter organisation became the means through which the state intervened in the management of industry. By 1939 the state had an interest in a range of large industrial concerns such as ILVA (steel) or Ansaldo (shipbuilding).

## Agriculture

- The state intervened in agriculture mainly for ideological reasons.
- Mussolini stated his desire to 'ruralise Italy'.
- The aim to be self-sufficient in wheat in times of war was the rationale for the '**Battle for Wheat**', started in 1925. Through the use of high tariffs on wheat (by 1933 it was 750 lire/ton) and improved farming techniques, such as the introduction of modern farm machinery, the production of wheat grew by around 50% between 1925–35. Consequently, the importation of foreign wheat fell by 75%.
- The government also intervened to subsidise **land reclamation**. Agriculture in the previous century had been blighted by malaria, the spread of which was encouraged by marshy land. Malaria was most common in the south where large areas were uninhabitable in the

summer, despite the fertility of the soil. Accordingly, the Liberal State had encouraged reclamation as part of the improvement of the countryside.

- The '**Mussolini Law**' of 1928 furthered this process by offering huge sums of state capital to finance suitable projects. In some areas this policy bore impressive results, such as the Pontine Marshes near Rome which were reclaimed for cultivation.

## Population

- In the 1920s the quota of Italian immigrants was cut by the USA, with the consequence that by the 1930s the yearly migration was only 5% of the 1910 figure. This caused overpopulation and internal migration, the population of Rome doubling between 1921–40 (with most of the migrants coming from the impoverished south).
- Such urbanisation was, in part, due to the effects of the '**Battle for Wheat**' which damaged the rural economy in the south, the land there being unsuitable for growing wheat. So, many peasants moved north to find work. This very much contradicted the fascist aim to 'ruralise' Italy.
- Closely linked to agricultural policy and this supposed 'ruralisation' was the regime's attempt to boost the birth rate. By a series of measures the state attempted to improve fertility. A bachelor tax, 'marriage loans', family allowances and employment preferment to people who were married with children were some of the measures introduced in the so called '**Battle for Births**'.

## Autarky

- So as to fulfil what he saw as Italy's imperial destiny, in 1935 Mussolini ordered the invasion of **Ethiopia**.
- This move provoked the imposition of **League of Nation sanctions**. These sanctions lasted until July 1936, although they did not prevent the sale of oil to Italy which would have been very damaging. However, the effect of sanctions was an even more pronounced policy of **autarky** (self-sufficiency). The problem was that such a protectionist policy meant even more government expenditure on top of campaigns in Ethiopia and intervention in the Spanish Civil War.
- In October 1936, the lire was devalued and one-off taxes on capital were introduced. Yet such considerations did not stop the expenditure. In 1937 Mussolini ordered an ambitious rearmament plan. In January 1938 a huge naval construction plan was introduced. By the eve of the Second World War, expenditure on the military accounted for around one-third of all state expenditure. An even more worrying statistic was that by 1938–39, the budget deficit was approaching 13 thousand million lire.

How to Pass AS Modern World History

### Relations with the Church

The resolution of the problem of **Church-State hostility** was to be one of the fascist regime's greatest successes.

- The hostility stemmed from the incorporation of Rome into the new Italian State in 1871, against the wishes of the Papacy. Initially there was considerable tension between the new fascist government and the Catholic Church.
- In 1925 attacks on Catholics and members of the **Popolari** (the main Catholic political party) by fascist squads provoked bitterness on both sides.
- This was followed in 1927 by the banning of certain Catholic youth groups.

However, it was in the interest of both Catholic Church and fascist state that some kind of settlement was made. For Pope Pius XI and the Church in general, the fascist government represented a bulwark against communist and socialist anti-clericalism. For Mussolini, recognition by the Church would provide the regime with the legitimacy it craved. The result was the negotiation and signing of the **Lateran Treaties** in 1929. This series of measures included:

- The creation of the Vatican as an independent state. The new state was given 44 hectares of land in the centre of Rome.
- A concordat regulated the activities of the Catholic Church, ensuring the survival of lay groups and accepting religious education in secondary schools. These were significant gains for the Papacy, especially when one considers the strength of anti-clerical legislation in the 1890s, as explained in the previous unit.
- The Papacy received an indemnity payment of 750 million lire, and one thousand million lire in state bonds as compensation for land lost before 1870.

This led to a less tense relationship between Church and State, although there was still some friction. In 1931 'Catholic Action', a Church youth organisation, was set up. Because it offered pastimes, such as sports, which closely matched the activities of fascist youth groups, it was partially suppressed.

The Catholic student organisation (FUCI) managed to prosper in these years. The popularity of Church education grew as state reforms altered the nature of Italian secondary education. The 1923 reforms of the Minister of Education, Giovanni Gentile, reduced the amount of technical education that was available, and stressed the importance of literature, philosophy and history. The introduction of a compulsory examination at the end of secondary schooling helped boost the numbers of students in Catholic secondary schools to around 100,000 in 1940 from approximately 30,000 in 1927.

## Leisure and popular culture

The regime attempted to promote its values through propaganda and leisure activities and, until 1936, this was relatively benign.

- In 1925 the **Opera Nazionale Dopolavoro (OND)** was set up to co-ordinate leisure activities. Known as the **Dopolavoro** (translated as 'after work'), its membership grew to 4 million by 1939, with members attracted in the main by the cheap holidays and the wide variety of recreation on offer. There is little doubt that the Dopolavoro was authentically popular, its activities taking in not only leisure but welfare.
- The fascists created the **Opera Nazionale Balilla** in 1926 to indoctrinate the young. Formed primarily as a militaristic organisation, it catered for all ages from 6 to 21. Again, membership became the norm.
- Until 1938, there was very little obvious opposition to the regime. In fact, conformity was very common, e.g. only 11 out of 1,200 university professors refused swear an oath to the fascist regime.
- State-dominated broadcasting was generally popular. The cinema was similarly enjoyed, despite being censored. From 1934 onwards it was funded by the state.
- The regime's control of the media was tightened from 1937 by the creation of the **Ministry of Popular Culture**.
- Sport served to reinforce the images that the media presented of a vibrant dynamic nation. In 1934 and 1938, the regime basked in the glory of successive football World Cup victories.

## The reform of customs, 1938

The late 1930s saw a change in the emphasis of the regime's social policy.

- In 1938 the **reform of customs** was introduced. This included an insistence on the use of the fascist salute, the widespread wearing of uniform and the Italianisation of English phrases.
- More sinister was the introduction of **anti-Semitic** legislation, despite a previously sympathetic attitude to Italy's 45,000 Jews. Following a press campaign and the issuing of a '**Manifesto of Racial Scholars**' by the Ministry of Popular Culture, the anti-Semitic laws were introduced on 3 August 1938. By this, all Jews who had taken up residence in Italy since 1919 were to leave within 6 months, Jewish teachers and students were barred from universities and schools, marriage was banned between Jews and non-Jews and Jews were forbidden to own substantial business interests or land.
- The measures resulted in the emigration of 6,000 Jews, but alienated many including academics, Church followers and business leaders in industry and banking, all of whom found such an application of fascist ideology repugnant. The regime also launched an attack on Italy's middle classes, e.g. death duties were increased in 1939.

How to Pass AS Modern World History

# Assessment: Italy, 1925–40

## Questions in the style of AQA (Unit 1)

Read the source and then answer the following questions.

Adapted from *The European Dictatorships 1918–1945*, by S Lee, 1987.

> Almost all the great personalities of the [inter-war] period were critics of democracy ... The masses were tempted by their charisma, sweeping promises and simple solutions.

**Q 1a What was meant by 'critics of democracy' in relation to the rise of Mussolini's regime?** (3)

### How to answer this question

The question asks you to develop an explanation of this phrase. You are to put this into the context of Mussolini's condemnation of the Liberal State as responsible for the 'mutilated victory' of Versailles, and into the context of the social and economic turmoil of the 1919–23 period.

**Q b Why did Mussolini establish a one-party state in Italy between 1925–39?** (7)

### How to answer this question

When answering this question, you are expected to:
- show that you understand a range of factors which help to explain the creation of a one-party state
- prioritise and explain the relative significance of the factors
- link the factors together
- challenge the question – candidates working at the highest level will argue that the one-party state was compromised by the continuing influence of the Church and establishment.

**Q c 'The role of Mussolini was the most important factor in the development of the one-party state in Italy in the period 1922–39.' Explain how far you agree with this statement.** (15)

### How to answer this question

The general rules for answering this type of question are given on pages 3–5. The question asks you to construct a balanced explanation of why a one-party state developed during the period stated. Because the question offers you one factor, in this case 'the role of Mussolini', you must explain the significance of that particular factor. However, you should make an evaluation of the relative influences of a range of factors. The following are examples of factors you might consider covering when explaining the nature of the Italian State between 1922–39:

- the role of Mussolini
- the fascist decrees of 1925–29
- the role of the Church and the establishment
- repression
- propaganda
- the failure of any opposition.

Here is part of an answer in which the student attempted to argue the role of the Church and its significance in the development of a one-party State.

> The Church gave its backing to the regime and the Lateran Treaties gave the fascist government enhanced legitimacy. The Lateran Treaties ensured that fascism would not be unchallenged. Although the support of the Church for Mussolini's one-party state boosted his standing both at home and abroad, it also meant that the Italy did not become a totalitarian State. Catholic Action and Catholic youth movements flourished as alternatives to the Balilla, membership standing at one million and just under 400,000 respectively by 1939. By 1940 one in every six secondary school students was being educated by the Church and not the state, and these were often the children of the middle classes. If education forms the basis of indoctrination, these figures reveal the extent to which the regime fell short. However, the existence of an alternative to the ideas of fascism may explain why the one-party state lasted as long as it did. Having an accepted alternative view from the Church meant that there was less need for an organised opposition.

## Further question in the style of AQA (Unit 1)

Read the source and then answer the following questions.

From *Modern Italy 1871-1982*, by M Clark, 1984.

> Thus Mussolini did not really seize power. He did not, by 28 October, need to use force......Mussolini won by being 'brought into the system' by a king that could see no other way of containing organised violence

Q  2a  **Explain what was meant by 'organised violence' in the context of Italy in the period 1918–22.**                    (3)
   b  **Why was Mussolini asked to be Prime Minister in 1922?**        (7)
   c  **How important was Mussolini in the consolidation of fascist power in Italy from 1922–29?**                         (15)

# Section 3: Italian foreign policy, 1924–45

## Corfu

One of the reasons why Mussolini came to power was the perceived humiliation of Versailles. Therefore, Mussolini was determined to follow a far more assertive foreign policy. In 1923 an Italian general and four of his staff were assassinated in Corfu. In response, the Italians bombed the island and then invaded it. Greece appealed to the League of Nations but it was the British who persuaded the Italians to leave the island after compensation had been promised.

## Fiume

In 1924 Mussolini managed to persuade Yugoslavia to recognise Fiume as Italian, which was an important symbolic triumph. A port on the frontier between Italy and the new Yugoslavia, Fiume had a largely Italian-speaking population. It was, therefore, claimed by Italian nationalists to be Italian.

By the Treaty of Rapallo of 1920, Fiume was declared an independent city. This was towards the end of nationalist Gabriele d'Annunzio's failed take-over of the city, which left it an even more potent symbol of Italian nationalism. Mussolini's success in 1924 boosted his personal standing considerably.

## Mussolini the diplomat

Throughout the 1920s and early 1930s, Mussolini fulfilled the role of a responsible European statesman.

- In 1925 he managed to present himself as a diplomat of stature by signing the Treaty of Locarno in person.
- In 1930, Italy signed a treaty at the end of the **London Naval Conference** which regulated naval warfare.
- In 1933, Italy played a leading role at the meeting of the **Disarmament Conference**, although plans to limit armament production were thwarted by objections from the new German government.
- In 1935, Mussolini attended the **Stresa Conference**. His commitment to Austrian independence, even at this time, shows that Mussolini was very much in tune with Britain and France against German expansion.
- It was Mussolini's belief that the greatest threat to Italy lay from a resurgent Germany and weakened Austria. For that reason he aimed to make an alliance with Austria and so in February 1930 Italy and Austria signed a treaty of friendship.
- In March 1934 the Rome Protocols were signed between Italy, Austria and Hungary. The protocols were designed to improve trade links and to create a group of countries to counterbalance French and German influence.

- In July 1930 Germany, Italy, Britain and France signed a **Four Power Pact**. The Pact merely reinforced commitments made in other recent treaties including Locarno. The driving force behind the pact was Mussolini who believed that such a powerful block of countries could replace the influence of the League of Nations. In reality the Pact was of virtually no significance. Yet Mussolini continued to keep close links with Britain and France as a means of containing Germany.

## Ethiopia

In January 1935 an agreement between France and Italy opened the way for an Italian invasion of Ethiopia.

- The French were willing to turn a blind eye to Italian expansion in Ethiopia in return for co-operation against Germany. Such co-operation was forthcoming the following April at the Stresa Conference. Italy wholeheartedly joined in the protests against German rearmament, but this issue was overshadowed by Italian actions in Ethiopia.
- The invasion of Ethiopia in October 1935 took place to fulfil Mussolini's colonial ambitions and partly to avenge Adowa.
- A clash of Italian and Ethiopian troops at **Wal-Wal** in December 1934 was seized upon by the Italians as the excuse to invade. Despite prolonged diplomatic efforts to avoid war, the invasion began in October 1935.
- Defeat for the Ethiopians was relatively swift as over half a million men were thrown into the conflict.
- Despite the application of sanctions voted by the League of Nations in November 1935, the Italian armies, commanded by General Bagdolio, had seized Addis Ababa by May 1936. The triumph for Mussolini was complete but it was won at a considerable financial and diplomatic cost, the estrangement from Britain and France having important long-term implications, as will be seen below.

## The Spanish Civil war and alliance with Germany

In 1937 Italian forces became heavily involved in the Spanish Civil War on the grounds that Italy could not 'permit' the establishment of a 'communist' government on the Mediterranean. However, Italian forces contributed little to the nationalist war effort, despite sending 75,000 troops and 1,400 pilots. In March 1937 they suffered the ultimate humiliation of defeat at the **Battle of Guadalajara** at the hand of an army with a heavy presence of Italian anti-fascist volunteers. Such involvement further distanced Italy from Britain and France and pushed her closer to alliance with Nazi Germany. This was foreseen by Mussolini who believed that the time was right for a readjustment in the balance of power in Europe.

- In October 1936 the Italy and Germany signed an agreement, the key

How to Pass AS Modern World History

point of which was a German promise to respect Austrian independence – despite Hitler's obvious designs on the country of his birth.

- In November 1937 Italy joined into an anti-communist pact with Germany and Japan. The following month she withdrew from the League of Nations.
- In March 1938 the Nazis engineered a crisis in Austria and invaded immediately. In April a plebiscite (vote) was held in which 99.75% of Austrians voted in favour of union with Germany (the vote being rigged). **Anschluss** (the German's 'union' with Austria) now brought Germany to Italy's borders, but Mussolini was powerless to intervene.
- Despite the threat that Anschluss posed in 1938 and despite a mending of relations with Britain which culminated in the Anglo-Italian Pact of November of that year, Italy concluded a close military alliance, the '**Pact of Steel**', with Germany in May 1939. Italy's commitments in Libya, Spain and Ethiopia made intervention impossible. This led to close co-operation between the two country's armed forces.

### The Second World War and defeat, 1939–45

The performance of the Italian economy and armed forces during the Second World War was dismal. Coupled with a collapse of morale on the home front, this somewhat dispels the view that the fascists had succeeded in transforming Italy into a militaristic nation. Italy was unprepared for war and the regime was horrified by the news of the German invasion of Poland in September 1939. To avoid humiliation, Italy remained neutral or 'non-belligerent'. **Neutrality** was widely welcomed in Italy, especially as the Germans had only recently signed a pact with Stalin's Soviet Union. By May 1940, however, the prospect of easy pickings with the imminent collapse of France, plus the fact that the regime's whole rationale was based on war, led to a declaration of hostilities against the allies. The King gave his consent to such a declaration, despite widespread opposition amongst the armed forces, establishment and the population at large. Mussolini was very much the driving force for war. The contradiction of Italian fascism was most apparent at this point. An ideology rooted in the concept of armed struggle was unprepared for and mostly unwilling to face its most important military challenge.

### Military failure

Italian military involvement in the war was constituted of a series of disasters:

- In October 1940 Mussolini's Army invaded Greece, only to suffer a series of reversals which resulted in the resignation of Marshal Bagdolio in December.
- The Italian Army was driven out of East Africa by the spring of 1941 and had to be rescued by German forces after being defeated in the North

African campaign by the British.

- Strategic errors and problems of supply simply lowered morale further amongst the armed forces and on the home front.
- In 1940 Mussolini had expected a rapid peace, but the fact that Italy did not join the war in 1939 reflected the concern that the armed forces were woefully under prepared. Tank production was far too small to supply Italy's supposed motorised divisions – only 667 tanks were produced in 1942 and 350 in 1943.

## Problems of supply

- The army received too few vehicles for transportation of men and materials, only around 80,000 vehicles between 1940–43. This constrained the tactical options of the army whose planned strategies were already extremely limited, as can be seen by the dismal failures in Greece and Africa in 1940–41.
- To make matters worse, production of armaments and war essentials actually fell during the war, e.g. in 1941 Fiat produced approximately half the number of vehicles it produced in 1938!
- The 227,000 soldiers on the Eastern Front were very badly equipped to fight any type of war. The reason for this was a shortage of fuel which reduced Italy's capacity to produce weapons.
- Whilst Italian steel production fell to 1.9 million tonnes in 1941, Russia was producing 25 million tonnes and the UK 14 million tonnes.

## Economic failure

The fascist regime failed to transform the Italian economy into one which was self-sufficient and could provide in times of war, in fact the opposite was true.

- As the war progressed, Italy became totally reliant on imports of oil from Romania and coal from Germany, and these supplies were both woefully insufficient. In practical terms it made all armed forces uncompetitive.
- The air force was expected to undertake the main burden of war in the Mediterranean as the Italian navy had no aircraft carriers. This was hampered by lack of aviation fuel.
- There was no co-ordination of the armed forces with often tragic results. In 1940 during the battle of Punta Stilo, Italian ships were bombed by their own air force.
- What is remarkable is that Italian economic policy before the war was geared to rearmament and autarky. This policy was a failure on a grand scale, despite 15 billion lire a year being spent on the military. On top of this failure was the fact that by 1939 the state had built up a crippling debt of 12.7 thousand million lire trying to achieve this. In particular, too much money was wasted on the colonisation of Ethiopia which brought Italy little gain. The efforts of the regime to transform the economy to support a war failed.

How to Pass AS Modern World History

The bureaucracy which developed as a result of the state interference in the economy in the 1930s placed a constraint on enterprise and development. The nature of economic development under the fascists resulted in cartels and mergers which produced monopolies such as Fiat, Olivetti and Pirelli. This limited the scope for innovation which was essential for a war economy, for example Italian aircraft such as the Fiat CR 42 were consistently outperformed by the Spitfire or Hurricane.

## Lack of support for the war

The lack of support for the Second World War in Italy from 1940–43 contrasts with the response in Germany or Britain to state propaganda. It is true that the fascist war aims were unclear and the early defeats in the war reduced morale. This was compounded by bombing which led to mass de-urbanisation – half a million people had left Milan by 1942. The strikes in Turin and elsewhere in 1943 were symptoms of a deeper discontent – they were partly aimed at the continuing war.

## Attitude of the Church

The Catholic Church maintained its independence and Pius XII's condemnation of aspects of the war in 1942 further undermined the regime. This again is a key point as it reflects the extent to which the regime failed to unite Italy behind the war. This was not an isolated incident, however. Throughout the war the Church's newspaper **Osservatore Romano** criticised the war and attracted a growing readership. In reality, fascism had failed fundamentally to transform society. Added to this, the Fascist Party itself was not prepared for war and crumbled in the face of public criticism and derision.

## Mussolini's dismissal

The growing crisis was reflected in Mussolini's dismissal of 11 Cabinet members in February 1943. The following month saw a series of strikes in industrial centres such as Turin which reflected the weakness of the regime. There is no doubt that the establishment which had brought Mussolini to power was actively conspiring to depose him from spring of that year. On 9 and 10 July, Sicily was invaded by the Allies and, far more significantly, Rome was bombed for two hours on 19 July. The fascist Grand Council, which had not met since 1939 was convened and criticised Mussolini. On 24 July the King dismissed Mussolini and had him arrested.

The government which replaced him was led by Marshall Bagdolio. Although Mussolini was restored to power in the North as leader of the ill-fated Republic of Salo, it was only as a puppet of the Germans. In April 1945 he was hanged in the Piazzale Loreto in Milan by the partisans.

# Assessment: Italian foreign policy, 1924–45

## Questions in the style of OCR (Unit 3)

**Q  1a  Explain the aims of Mussolini's foreign policy in the period 1924–39.**                                                      (30)

### How to answer this question

To answer this question you need to ensure that you cover the range of the period in question. It is essential that you plan your answer effectively by isolating the different themes of Mussolini's foreign policy in the 1920s and 30s. Here are some factors you might like to consider which should be mentioned in a top quality answer:
* expansion of the Italian Empire
* achieving 'great power' status
* dominance of the Mediterranean.

Here is an extract from an answer to the question. Note how the candidate has attempted to prioritise in his/her answer.

> The most important aim of Mussolini's foreign policy was to achieve great power status for Italy. This was a reflection of the insecurity felt post Versailles. It led Italy into the Spanish Civil War in 1937 as Mussolini attempted to influence the outcome of events abroad through use of arms. In believing his own propaganda that Italy had become a great power by the mid-1930s, Mussolini was led into a series of foreign policy mistakes. He thought that by allying with Germany from 1936 he could drag concessions from Britain and France over Africa and the Balkans – this was a miscalculation.

**Q  b  Explain why Mussolini was overthrown in 1943.**                                                      (60)

### How to answer this question

It is wise to plan a line of analysis before you embark on your answer. As you are asked to compare, it is important that you work out in your own mind the links between the factors and their respective importance. In particular, you need to work out which is the most important.

Here are examples of some key points you might put in your plan.
* Mussolini's downfall was primarily the result of military failure which discredited the regime. However, this failure is strongly linked to the failure of the regime's economic policy of autarky.
* The establishment was responsible for the dismissal of Mussolini in that the King reflected wider concerns about Italy's imminent defeat.

Here is an example of an extract from an answer which attempts to:
- analyse the importance of the contributions of each of three reasons for Mussolini's downfall
- link the factors of military defeat and economic failure to Mussolini's downfall.

> The fascist regime failed to transform the Italian economy into one which was self-sufficient and could provide in times of war. As the war progressed, Italy became totally reliant on imports of oil from Romania and coal from Germany, and these were both insufficient. Tank production was far too small to supply Italy's supposed motorised divisions – only 667 tanks were produced in 1942 and 350 in 1943. This compares poorly with the other major combatants – in Britain 8611 and 7476 tanks were produced in these 2 years respectively. Similarly, the Army received too few vehicles for transportation of men and materials, only around 80,000 vehicles between 1940–43. This constrained the tactical options of the Army whose planned strategies were already extremely limited, as can be seen by the failures in Greece and Africa in 1940–41. In practical terms, it made all armed forces uncompetitive. What is remarkable is that Italian economic policy before the war was geared to rearmament and autarky. This policy was a failure on a grand scale, despite 15 billion lire a year being spent on the military. The regime was based on the ideal of transforming Italy into a country capable of sustaining war. When this was proved to be a facade, so support for the regime weakened, in particular amongst the establishment and, importantly, the King.

## Further question in the style of OCR (Unit 3)

Q   2a   **Identify and explain the reasons why Mussolini forged closer diplomatic links with Nazi Germany in the period 1936-39.**                                  (30)

   b   **To what extent could Mussolini's foreign and colonial policy from 1925-43 be called a success?**                                  (60)

# Chapter 5
# Germany, 1918–45

## Section 1: The democratic experiment – Weimar Germany, 1918–24

### The threat from the extremes of left and right

- As Germany faced defeat in early November 1918 German sailors based at the ports of Wilhelmshaven and Kiel refused orders to go to sea to fight the British. On 4 and 5 November 1918, the mutiny spread to other ports.
- In Berlin there were calls in the Reichstag for the Kaiser, **Wilhelm II**, to abdicate.
- Councils of workers and soldiers (soviets) were set up in Rostock, Bremen and other towns.
- In Munich, a revolt headed by socialist Kurt Eisner led to the proclamation of a Republic in Bavaria.
- On 9 November Wilhelm abdicated. The most powerful political group in Germany was now the **SPD** (Social Democratic Party) led by **Friedrich Ebert** and **Philipp Scheidemann**.
- On 11 November German delegates met with representatives of the Allies at Compiegne and signed the agreement that ended 4 years of war.

### The Spartacist revolution

The new German Chancellor Friedrich Ebert faced an even more pressing problem at home. Extreme left-wing groups in Germany rejected any democratic Parliament and were pressing for a revolution. At the end of 1918 the greatest threat came from the **Spartacist Union** led by Karl Liebknecht and Rosa Luxemburg. Their aims were:
- the cancellation of the National Assembly and transfer of all power to soldier and worker councils, and militias
- seizure of all large and medium farms, as well as large industrial companies, with state control of coal, iron and steel industries .

The Spartacists' policies and direct tactics frightened the SPD-led government who looked to the Army to keep order.
- On 9 November, Chancellor Ebert had a conversation with a leading figure in the Army, **General Gröner**, who promised army support against revolution and loyalty to the new government.
- On 5 January the Spartacists attempted a revolt in Berlin. However, the uprising was poorly organised and was crushed by the government using the **Reichswehr** and **Freikorps** troops led by General Walther von

How to Pass AS Modern World History

Lüttwitz. On 15 January, members of the Horse Guards Division of the army murdered Karl Liebknecht and Rosa Luxemburg.

- For Ebert to use the Reichswehr against his enemies on the left was a political mistake. Many of the army's officers and soldiers were anti-democratic and against the Republic.
- The leader of the army from 1920–26, **General Hans von Seeckt** developed the idea of the army working as a 'state within a state', i.e. the interests of the army were more important than those of the state.
- The army was unreliable as a law enforcer. It did little to stop the work of murder squads and the political violence which resulted in the murder of Weimar politicians Walther Rathenau and Matthias Erzberger, and over 200 others.
- In February and March 1919 forces directed by Defence Minister Gustav Noske crushed uprisings in Berlin and Munich. A more serious challenge came from the establishment of a Soviet Republic in Bavaria in April 1919. The Reichswehr and the Freikorps also crushed this rebellion.

## The Treaty of Versailles

The most important issue facing the new state was the peace treaty drawn up by the victorious powers at Versailles. The German delegation that went to Versailles was not permitted to take part in the negotiations. In May 1919 the terms of the treaty were presented to a horrified Germany. There was considerable resentment at the 'war guilt' clause and the fact that the treaty was harsher than **Wilson's Fourteen Points** had originally suggested. Rather than accept the treaty, Philipp Scheidemann's Cabinet resigned to be replaced by one led by Gustav Bauer of the SPD. A new government was formed and on 28 June the Foreign Minister **Hermann Müller** and Minister of Communications **Johannes Bell** signed the Treaty of Versailles.

The Versailles settlement.
- Germany was humiliated as a great power.
- She lost territory of economic importance (producing up to 20% of coal production and 15% of agricultural resources), as well as territory of symbolic importance such as West Prussia. It was this loss of land to Poland which perhaps caused the greatest upset in Germany as most people in West Prussia and Posen were German speakers.
- Germany's military capability was destroyed – the army being limited to 100,000 men and the navy to six ships.
- One of the most unpopular aspects of the treaty in Germany was Article 231 in which Germany accepted full responsibility for causing the war. The rationale for this article was to establish the principle of German liability which could lead to compensation (**reparations**) being paid to the Allies. However, such a judgement became quickly widened into a moral question of the extent of Germany's supposed 'war guilt'. The

politicians of the Republic who were faced with this clause, attempted to have it dropped from the final treaty. The Allies, however, were in no mood to compromise, and on 28 June 1919 the treaty was signed.

## Results of the Versailles Treaty

- Versailles left Germany humiliated and scarred, but she was still potentially strong. There was disillusion in Germany because she had been excluded from the League of Nations – but according to the treaty, Germany remained a United Nation State with the potential to regain her status as an important diplomatic power. This was proved by the Treaty of Rapallo in 1922 between Germany and the Soviet Union.
- **'Stab in the back'**. As part of the discussions on the treaty in Germany the leading generals, including General Hindenberg, advised that the German army was in no state to resist the Allies militarily. However in November 1919, Hindenberg gave evidence to the Investigation Committee of the National Assembly. His testimony backed up the views of the right-wing parties and press that Versailles was a humiliating and shameful peace (*Schmachfrieden*) which should not have been signed. Hindenberg and his political allies denounced the so-called 'November criminals' who founded the Republic. They were also blamed for the 'stab in the back' of the armed forces that led to military collapse in 1918. Such theories were very useful to the anti-Republican right.

## The Weimar Constitution

The authors of the Constitution adopted in July 1919 attempted to build on the traditions of German politics, as well as balance power between the different institutions of the state.

- The new Constitution created the **Reich** (State) as a **parliamentary democracy**, with the Chancellor and Cabinet requiring majority support in the **Reichstag** (the Parliament).
- The Constitution provided for a strong executive with a **President** elected on a 7-year cycle and with strong counterbalancing powers against the legislature (the Reichstag). The President could dissolve the Reichstag and could block new laws by calling a referendum. Most importantly, by Article 48, the President could suspend the Reichstag and rule by decree in the case of 'national emergency'. The **Reich Chancellor** led the German government, being accountable to the Reichstag.
- The new Parliament was to be made up of two houses: the **Reichsrat** which had the power to delay laws (its members were chosen by the Parliaments of the **Länder**) and the Reichstag for which elections were to be held every 4 years. The constitution introduced proportional representation voting for the Reichstag, which had a strong influence on the nature of politics in the years ahead. It led to **coalition governments** that rose and fell with spectacular consistency. However, in 1919 the

How to Pass AS Modern World History

introduction of proportional representation was accepted by most across the political spectrum.

- All men and women over the age of 20 were able to vote.
- The **Bill of Rights** guaranteed individual rights such as freedom of speech and the right to belong to a union.

## Kapp Putsch, 1920

- Amongst those on the political right most violently opposed to the Weimar Republic were General Ludendorff and monarchist Wolfgang Kapp, who formed the **National Association** in October 1919 to raise support for their cause. A leading member of the Freikorps, General von Lüttwitz, joined them in their conspiracy.
- In March 1920, the government ordered the disbanding of the **Ehrhardt Marine Brigade** who were stationed in Berlin. Von Lüttwitz rejected the disbandment and, on 13 March, used 5000 troops from the brigade to seize government buildings in Berlin.
- Only the Commander in Chief of the Army, General Reinhardt, was prepared to use force against the uprising, but all other commanders were unwilling to release troops. The putsch collapsed because the trade unions called a General Strike and the cautious Civil Service refused to accept Kapp's orders.

## The aftermath of the Kapp Putsch

The government did not move against its opponents in the army. It appointed Hans von Seeckt Head of the Army Command, despite his refusal to allow his troops to be used to put down the uprising. The main reason why the government didn't act was because the Kapp Putsch had set off a wave of strikes and communist-inspired uprisings across the country. On 19 March a huge Spartacist revolt took place in the mining region of the Ruhr. A new Cabinet was formed by Hermann Müller in late March 1920 which used von Seeckt's Army to put down the Ruhr uprising in April. The significance of the Kapp Putsch is that it worsened the division between the right-wing groups and the Republic.

## Further violence

- In March 1921 the Army and police crushed KPD (Communist party) uprisings in Hamburg and central Germany. Although the Freikorps had been disbanded, right-wing groups sustained a programme of political violence.
- The socialist leader Karl Gareis was shot in June 1921 as was Matthias Erzberger two months later.
- In June 1922 right-wing extremists shot the Foreign Minister Walther Rathenau.
- Although political violence was not confined to the actions of the right,

354 out of the 376 political murders were attributed to them rather than their political opponents.

### Elections of 1920

- Elections for the Reichstag were held in the aftermath of the Kapp Putsch.
- The main 'Weimar Coalition' parties of the SPD (Socialist Democratic Party), Centre and DDP (Democratic Party) suffered heavy losses. Before the coalition commanded 78% of the seats in the National Assembly. Now it dominated only 45% of the Reichstag.
- The result of the failure of the mainstream parties to gain a majority was that the parties who supported the Republic were weakened.
- Government was also weakened as it became dominated by a series of coalitions opposed by parties such as the DNVP (National Party), USPD (Independent Socialists), and KPD. Virtually straight away the new coalition government, led by Konstantin Fehrenbach, faced the problem of reparations.

### Reparations and Versailles

By Article 231 of the Versailles Treaty, Germany was made responsible for the war and thereby liable to pay reparations to the Allies. On 1 May 1921 the victorious powers finally set reparations at 20,000 billion gold marks. This agreement was known as the **London Payments Plan** and instructed a payment of 2,000 gold marks a year plus 26% of the value of Germany's exports. On 4 May the Fehrenbach government resigned rather than accept these demands. It was replaced by a government led by Joseph Wirth who was also from the Centre Party. The Allies had little sympathy with German claims of economic problems and by the London Ultimatum of 5 May they threatened to invade the Ruhr unless the Germans agreed to their demands. On 11 May but against bitter opposition from nationalists, Wirth agreed to accept the demands for reparations under the policy of fulfilment.

### Financial collapse and the Ruhr crisis, 1922–23

- By the middle of 1922 the main problem for the German State was an unstable currency, because of the effects of the war. By 1919 the national debt was 144,000 million marks. Reparations made matters worse.
- In July 1922 the government asked for permission to suspend reparation payments but the Allies refused. Germany also declared that they would be unable to make reparation payments in 1923 and 1924.
- By December 1922 the national debt was 469,000 million marks.
- A new centre-right government led by Wilhelm Cuno had taken office in November 1922 but it also faced a disastrous financial situation. At the end of the year, the Reparations Commission declared that Germany had failed to deliver promised coal and timber to the Allies.

- The response of the French was to occupy the Ruhr with Belgian support. On 11 January 1923 French engineers were sent into the Ruhr to secure production of coal. They were backed up by 60,000 French and Belgian soldiers. Cuno's government encouraged the workers and population of the Ruhr to offer '**passive resistance**' and it ordered the immediate suspension of reparations payments. The policy of 'passive resistance' worked in that the amount of coal delivered to France and Belgium was considerably reduced.
- The cost to Germany was great. The government had to pay out millions of marks to those who had lost revenue as a result of 'passive resistance'.
- The denial of vital revenue from this area and all the other financial pressures resulted in the government issuing more notes. By August 1923 there were 663 billion marks in circulation leading to **hyperinflation**. In December 1922 the exchange rate stood at 8,000 marks to the dollar, by November 1923 it had reached 4.2 billion.
- As the currency collapsed so did the policy of 'passive resistance'. The collapse had a hugely damaging effect on whole swathes of society, making savings, pensions, government loans, mortgages and many salaries worthless. The middle classes suffered terribly as did German labour – by the end of 1923 only 29.3% of trade unions members worked full time. The currency had collapsed and with it all confidence in the German financial system.

## Stabilisation of the currency

In August 1923, a new government led by Gustav Stresemann was formed. It began to take measures to stabilise the situation.
- In September 1923 payments of reparations were resumed and in November 1923 the **Rentenmark** was established by the Finance Minister Hans Luther to replace the old mark.
- Further measures were taken to balance the budget including the sacking of 700,000 state employees.
- In November a **Rentenbank** was opened and **Hjalmar Schacht** was appointed Special Currency Commissioner with the task of replacing the worthless currency with the Rentenmark.

## Continuing unrest, 1923

There was still unrest on the extreme edges of politics.
- In October 1923 a KPD-planned uprising, the 'German October', was crushed before it started in Saxony and Thuringia.
- In Hamburg the uprising was easily defeated. The use of the army to crush it offended the socialist SPD to the extent that it left the government. The following month an attempted NSDAP (Nazi) putsch in Munich, led by a certain Adolf Hitler, was contained by the police.

# Assessment: The democratic experiment – Weimar Germany, 1918–24

## Questions in the style of Edexcel (Unit 2)

Q 1a Describe how the Weimar Republic (government and Constitution) was created in 1918–19. (15)

### How to answer this question

You are being asked to give a detailed explanation of the important features of the Weimar government and its Constitution in the years following the First World War. The key to answering this question effectively is to plan your answer thoroughly before you start writing. Even though the question is asking you to describe, you will still need a theme around which to base your ideas.

Firstly, you need to identify the themes which will help you answer the question. In this case it is clear that the question requires you to show an understanding of the nature of the new government and the Weimar Constitution. Here are examples of themes which you might use:

- The new government emerged from the abdication and the considerable unrest at the end of the war.
- The Weimar Constitution reflected the pre-war party system fought through proportional representation. It was more democratic, although it centralised power.

The next stage is to draw up a brief paragraph-by-paragraph plan, which will help you to structure your work. For example:

- **paragraph 1** – The abdication, creation of National Assembly
- **paragraph 2** – The need for stability because of external threats shaping the terms of the Constitution
- **paragraph 3** – Description of constitution.

Here is an example of an answer in which the candidate describes the powers of the Reichspresident.

> The Constitution gave quite considerable power to the Reichspresident. Most significant was the power given by Article 48 to rule by decree and without the Reichstag in times of national emergency. The aim of the authors of the Constitution was clear. By insisting that the President be elected directly by the people, for a period in office of just seven years, by giving him the power to disband the Reichstag and dismiss the government, they created a counterbalance to any potential 'elected Parliamentary dictatorship'. There had been no tradition in Germany before 1914 of a strong Reichstag. The creation of a strong President was

an attempt at creating political continuity. Ebert used Article 48 as an instrument for the preservation of the Republic, the best example being in November 1923 when he used it to give power to the army to put down the Munich Putsch.

## Q b Why was Germany politically unstable in the period 1918–23?

(15)

### How to answer this question

This is a question about causation. Therefore, you need to concentrate on the causes of the Republic's instability. The question demands a straightforward analytical answer. You must identify your main points of argument before you start. You should avoid simply listing the events of the period, although you will need the information to back up your main points. To gain top marks, try to prioritise what you think is the most important reason for instability.

Here are some ideas for lines of argument you could use in response to this question.
- The main threat to the stability of the Republic was the repeated attacks from its internal enemies on the left and right. The greater threat came from the forces of right-wing nationalism – those who despised the new democracy.
- One should not underestimate the psychological effects of the economic problems of 1918–23. Unemployment and financial insecurity undermined confidence in the political structure.
- Instability of the Republic was due to the actions of those who attempted to use the Treaty of Versailles to damage the new democracy.

In your introduction, you should use the main points of your argument to sum up the line you are going to take. Your first paragraph should be based on the main point of your argument. This argument should be backed up with carefully selected evidence. Here is an example of a clear style in an answer which addresses the question directly and uses evidence to back the arguments.

Political stability of any governmental system relies on the loyalty of key institutions. In the Weimar Republic, the Reichswehr in particular was instinctively anti-democratic. Many of its leading officers, including Hindenberg, promoted the idea of the 1918 'stab in the back'. However, it retained influence as a result of the fact that Ebert and his colleagues turned to the Reichswehr as the means by which forces of moderate Socialism could defeat the more radical left, such as the Spartacists in

1919. In the spring of 1919 the Reichswehr was used extensively to end strikes and to shut down the so-called 'Republics of Councils' created in cities such as Munich. But the forces of law and order were not reliable and their actions increased instability. The Army did little to stop the work of murder squads and the political violence which resulted in the murder of Weimar politicians Rathenau, Erzberger and over 200 others. Similarly the Reichswehr and police forces did little to hound the militarily-styled right-wing associations which were their successors. The Kapp Putsch of 1920 was orchestrated by leading military figures, including General von Lüttwitz. It had the widespread support of the military and it was the reaction of labour rather than the Army which led to its defeat. So the anti-Weimar attitude of many in the Reichswehr was crucial in creating political instability in the period in question.

## Further questions in the style of Edexcel (Unit 2)

Q  2a  Describe the challenge to the Weimar Republic from the Left and the Right in the years 1918–23. (15)

b  Why did Germany suffer economic and financial instability in the years 1918-24? (15)

Q  3a  Describe and explain the main features of the Weimar constitution. (15)

b  Explain why the treaty of Versailles aroused such opposition in Germany. (15)

# Section 2: Germany, 1923–29

### Gustav Stresemann as Foreign Minister 1923–29

Stresemann's foreign policy aims were as follows.

- He wanted to see a revision of the Treaty of Versailles. To achieve this revision he believed in fulfilment, agreeing to co-operate with the Allies in order to show that the Treaty was unworkable.
- Stresemann believed that guaranteeing French security was the key issue to better diplomatic relations.

### Stresemann and the Dawes Plan

Stresemann believed that fulfilment was Germany's best course of action in dealing with the Allies. In his view, Germany's greatest need was raw materials, new markets for her goods and new sources of capital and a restoration of confidence in her economy. To this end he encouraged the creation of the Dawes Committee which was a group of economists and other experts chaired by the American banker **Charles Dawes**. Their aim was to find a solution to the reparations problem under the slogan 'Business not politics'. In April 1924 the committee produced its report.

- The plan suggested that the French leave the Ruhr and that further sanctions be harder to apply.
- Reparations would be paid over a longer period and credit would be advanced to help rebuild the German economy. In the first years, an international loan of 800 million marks would be granted to cover four-fifths of the reparation payments. The higher level of 2,500 million marks a year set by the London Plan would be paid after 1929.
- The Reichsbank would be reorganised under Allied supervision.

### Better relations with the Allies, 1924–25

After the antagonism in relations between Germany and the Allied powers over the Ruhr, 1924 saw a significant change in attitudes on all sides.

- The election of a Labour government under Ramsay MacDonald in Britain in January 1924 produced a more conciliatory line towards Germany.
- Stresemann's position was strengthened by a change in French attitudes in the wake of the Ruhr occupation of 1923. Although the primary aim of the French in 1923 was to maintain security, the international backlash against their aggression resulted in a more conciliatory policy towards Germany, in particular in the wake of a victory for the left in the French elections of May 1924.

The change in emphasis could be seen in the diplomatic events of 1925. In April 1925 Aristide Briand became French Foreign Minister. He accepted the British suggestion that some kind of pact be signed to secure France's eastern borders. Months of negotiations followed which ended in the meetings at **Locarno** in October 1925.

## The Locarno Treaties, 1925

The Locarno Treaties were signed on 1 December:
- A treaty of mutual guarantee of the Franco-German and Belgo-German borders was signed with Britain and Italy verifying the agreement.
- All parties agreed not to use force to alter these frontiers.
- A series of arbitration treaties were signed at Locarno between Germany and France, Poland, Czechoslovakia and Belgium.

Stresemann held out against a Locarno-style settlement for Germany's eastern borders, hoping for revision of them at a later date. Not only was he successful, but he managed to secure guarantees from France that it would not attack Germany in the event of a war with Poland in which Germany was not the aggressor. Soon after the treaties, the first evacuation from the Rhineland took place in 1925. However, despite further talks on the subject between Stresemann and the French Foreign Minister Aristide Briand in September 1926, there was no more movement on that issue until 1929.

## Diplomatic improvements, 1925–6

The post-Locarno period up to 1929 saw an improvement in Germany's diplomatic situation.
- As part of the Locarno agreements, Germany was admitted to the **League of Nations** on 8 September 1926. It was agreed at the talks that, although she was granted a permanent seat on the Council, she was free from the military obligations as laid out in Article 16.
- In April 1926, the **Treaty of Berlin** was signed between the Soviet Union and Germany – this reaffirmed the Treaty of Rapallo of 1922 and stressed each country's neutrality in the event of attack by a third power.
- Relations between Germany and the western powers continued to improve. In late 1926, the Allied occupation forces in Germany were cut by a further 60,000. In January 1927 the Allies finally withdrew the **Inter-Allied Military Commission** (IMCC) which had been set up to oversee German disarmament as demanded by the Versailles Treaty.
- A commercial treaty was signed between France and Germany in August 1927. However, some tensions did remain with France which were heightened by Hindenburg's speech on 18 September of the same year, in which he denied Germany's war guilt and repudiated Article 231.

## The Young Plan

This plan dealt with the issue of reparations which re-emerged in 1929 because, under the Dawes Plan, Germany was due to start paying the higher rate of reparations. In September 1928, Germany asked France for a speedy evacuation of the Rhineland. The French, however, insisted that the issue of the Rhineland be linked to that of reparations. The Young Plan made the following points.

- For the first time, the time scale for reparation repayment was set; Germany was to make payments for the next 59 years until 1988. She was to pay 2,000 million marks a year instead of the 2,500 million marks as laid down by the Dawes Plan.
- Responsibility for paying reparations was to be given to Germany.
- Payments were to increase gradually and from 1929–32 Germany was to pay 1,700 million Reichmarks less than she would have paid under the Dawes Plan.
- If Germany agreed to the plan, the French promised to evacuate the Rhineland by June 1930, 5 years ahead of schedule. This was an important victory for Stresemann.

## Political instability and the collapse of Luther's coalition

- In December 1924, a new election brought a revival in the fortunes of the SPD, gaining 31 seats (mainly at the expense of the KPD who lost 17 seats).
- The new coalition government of January 1925 led by Hans Luther excluded the socialists but included members of the nationalist DNVP for the first time. This was to prove the undoing of the government as the DNVP objected to the terms of the Locarno Treaties negotiated by Stresemann and they were only ratified with support from the SPD in December 1925.
- A new coalition was sought but the SPD still objected to joining a coalition with 'bourgeois parties' (i.e. the DDP, Centre or DVP). This belief was strengthened by the adoption of a Marxist-based series of policies by the **Heidleburg programme** of 1925. Such a rejection of political responsibility weakened the whole process of democracy.
- On 26 April, General Hindenberg was elected President of the Weimar Republic. From the start of his presidency, Hindenburg made it clear that he would not accept SPD participation in a coalition government.

## Government instability, January 1926–February 1928

- In January 1926, Hans Luther formed a minority coalition involving the Centre Party, DVP and DNP but this Cabinet was not to last for long. The Reichstag passed a vote of no confidence in May 1926.
- **Wilhelm Marx** replaced Luther as Chancellor. On 20 June 1926 a referendum took place on the confiscation of royal property, the vote failing to reach the required majority. The Marx Cabinet relied on the support of the same parties as its predecessor and until late 1926 had the tacit support of the SPD. That support was removed in late 1926 and the Cabinet fell.

- In January 1927 another Wilhelm Marx-led government was formed. This time it included the nationalist DNVP. There was always a strain on the Cabinet, the interests of the DVP (People's Party), BVP and DNVP parties often being different. Nevertheless some important social legislation was passed, including a comprehensive reform of unemployment insurance in July 1927.
- The coalition collapsed in February 1928 over the issue of religion in education.

## The Reichstag election of May 1928

The election of May 1928 was an important turning point for the Weimar Republic:
- The left made important gains, the SPD increasing its share of the seats by 22 to 152 and the KPD showing a rise of 9 seats to 54.
- More significantly, as the parties of the centre and right saw their share of the vote drop, so there was a rise in the vote of splinter parties such as the Bauernbund (23 seats and 4.5% of the vote) which represented farmers' interests.
- The vote for the NSDAP in this election fell to 2.6%.

## Müller's Grand Coalition, 1928–30 and the Young Plan.

In June 1928 a ministry dominated by socialists was formed, led by **Hermann Müller** of the SPD. However, this new coalition was broad-based as it included members of the SPD, DDP, DVP, Centre and BVP. The main task of the so-called 'Grand Coalitions' was to steer the Young Plan through the Reichstag in 1929.

However, events were becoming overshadowed by the collapse of the New York stock exchange in October 1929. Much of the economic recovery of the mid-1920s had relied on short-term loans from abroad. As the Depression deepened, those who had lent money now demanded repayment. The most obvious problem was the growth in unemployment. By February 1929 17.7% of the population was unemployed. The growing crisis was to stretch and then break the 'Grand Coalition' over the issue of unemployment insurance. As unemployment began to rise, so the Reich Institution – in charge of unemployment benefits – had to borrow from the government to pay out benefits. By late 1929 it had borrowed 342 million Reichsmarks and put a strain on the government's budget. The coalition partners had different ideas on how to address the problem.
- The **SPD** believed that contributions to the fund to help the unemployed should be increased. It argued that central and local governments, employers and those on fixed wages should pay 4% more to help the unemployed.
- The **DVP** disagreed and argued that contributions should not be increased. Instead they believed that benefits should be cut.

- The Centre Party negotiated a deal whereby a decision on the issue would be put off until the autumn of 1930. In March 1930 SPD deputies rejected this compromise and brought down the socialist-led Müller government. The SPD had given up power and the move led to the formation of the **Brüning** Cabinet in March 1930.

## The economy 1924–29

- **Foreign investment**. Between 1924–29 there was monetary stability which was particularly important to those classes that had suffered because of the hyperinflation of 1923. This was due to the establishment of the Rentenmark and the effects of the Dawes Plan. As a result of the Dawes Plan, there was a significant influx of foreign capital, around 25.5 billion marks between 1924–30. The vast majority of this capital came from the USA and it enabled the reconstruction of German industry to take place.
- **Delay of reparation payments**. The growth in available capital in Germany was also due to the delaying of reparation payments at the highest rate as suggested by the Dawes Plan, thereby leading to investment in the German economy. As a result, national income was 12% higher in 1928 than in 1913 and industry experienced spectacular growth rates.
- **Unemployment**. Unemployment figures support the view that many of the economic problems may have had their roots in the supposed years of stability, e.g. in late 1928 the figure for those without work stood at 14.5% of the workforce.
- **Labour disputes**. In 1923, the legislation of 1918 that enforced an 8-hour day was altered to allow employers to institute a 10-hour day in some circumstances. Employers resisted the union demands for higher wages in this period, to the extent that between 1924–32 around 76,000 cases were brought to arbitration. There is little doubt that employers increasingly resented having to use such a procedure and in late 1928 over 210,000 workers in the Ruhr were locked out because the ironworks' owners would not accept the findings of arbitration.

# Assessment: Germany, 1923–29

## Course essay question in the style of AQA (Unit 3)

**Q 1** Examine the extent of economic prosperity and political stability in the Weimar Republic between 1923–29.

## How to answer this question

You are being asked to make a judgement about economic prosperity and political stability in the period stated. You should develop an argument which you can follow throughout your answer. You also need to select appropriate evidence to incorporate into your answer.

Because this is a course essay which will be written to time, you need to prepare a detailed but clear plan including both argument and content. Before you decide on the content you are going to use, you should identify the key points of your argument.

1 Economic prosperity was mainly due to the Dawes Plan and the influx of foreign capital. However, economic problems still existed in the late 1920s.

2 The political stability of the years in question was only relative to the years which preceded and followed. Successive coalition governments, the attitude of the SPD and the election of Hindenberg all meant that the weaknesses in the political system were not removed.

3 The most obvious factor which promoted political stability was the work of Stresemann as Foreign Minister.

You would be expected to cover both the economy and politics during this period. Here is some of the content which would be expected in work at the highest level.

- **Economy** Dawes Plan, economic growth, monetary stability, reparations, economic problems, labour unrest, unemployment.
- **Politics** Coalition governments, government instability, attitude of the SPD, Hindenberg as President, 'Grand Coalition', Stresemann's foreign policy.

Your style should be as direct as possible. Here is an extract from a top quality answer to this question.

So it is difficult to claim that this was a period of political stability, indeed the actions of the leading politicians helped discredit the Republic. The reluctance of the SPD to join coalitions was made worse by President Hindenburg's attempts to exclude them from influence in government. Such actions were to help create an atmosphere in which constructive political agreement was at best unlikely. Consensus was essential if the Republic was to tackle the political and economic problems it faced. However, from the moment of his election as President in 1926, Hindenburg worked tirelessly to create coalitions which would exclude the SPD. Therefore, many governments found it difficult to build working coalitions. When the socialists were included in government, e.g. the Müller government which was formed in June 1928, the government was beset with problems. Many within the DVP and Centre parties shared Hindenburg's reluctance to accept SPD dominance of a government, despite the fact that they were by far the largest party in the Reichstag. The result was the absence of a political consensus on how to deal with the country's growing unemployment and political challenges.

## Questions in the style of Edexcel (Unit 2)

For advice on how to answer questions of this type use the examples given on pages 95–7.

Q   2a  **Describe how Stresemann improved Germany's diplomatic position in the period 1924–29.**                                      (15)
     b  **Why did the German economy stabilise in the period 1924–29?**                                                      (15)

Q   3a  **In what could Germany be described as stable in the period 1924–29?**                                              (15)
     b  **Why were the Dawes Plan and the Locarno Treaties so important to stability in Germany in the period 1924–29?**   (15)

## Question in the style of AQA course essay (Unit 3)

Q   4  **Examine the importance of President Hindenberg in determining the political development of the Weimar Republic.**

# Section 3: The rise of the Nazi Party, 1919–33

## Introduction

The Nazi Party was founded by **Anton Drexler** in January 1919 as the **German Workers' Party**. It assumed its new name, the **National Socialist German Workers' Party** (NSDAP) and a 25-point programme at Munich in February 1920. Included in this manifesto, written by Drexler and Hitler, were themes that remained constant throughout the 1920s and beyond.

- **Revision of the Treaty of Versailles** This was to include an end to reparations. In wanting to revise the Treaty of Versailles, the Nazis intended to scrap article 231 by which Germany accepted guilt for the war.
- **Citizenship** The right to citizenship of the German State was only to be given to those of German blood. To the Nazis this automatically excluded Jews.
- **Lebensraum** 'Living space' was to be created for the German people.
- **Government** The creation of a strong government.
- **War profiteering** Making money from war was to be made a criminal offence.
- **Commerce** Large department stores were to be divided up and leased to small traders.

## The early years

In the following 3 years, Hitler consolidated his leadership of and influence on the Party, becoming Chairman of the Party in July 1921. This was followed by the creation of the SA, which was to become the paramilitary wing of the Party. On 8 and 9 November 1923 the Nazis attempted a violent coup. Known as the **Munich Putsch**, it was in many ways a farcical failure.

- On the evening of 8 November, Hitler and 600 SA soldiers stormed a public meeting in Munich, Hitler declaring that 'the national revolution has broken out'.
- The following day Hitler, Hermann Göring, Julius Streicher and General Ludendorff led a march into the centre of Munich, only to find their way barred by the police.
- Sixteen Nazis were killed in a brief street battle in which the Nazis were humiliated.

Hitler turned defeat into a kind of triumph.

- His trial for high treason in February–March 1924 was transformed into a propaganda coup by giving him and his comrades a nation-wide platform for their beliefs.
- The sympathy of the judges ensured he received the minimum term of 5 years imprisonment.

- Imprisoned in Landsberg Castle in 1924, Hitler wrote **Mein Kampf** ('My Struggle') which was to become his enduring political testament. In the book Hitler developed his **Weltanschauung** (world view or outlook).

## Party reorganisation

In May 1924, the Nazis, in alliance with other parties of the right, won 1.9 million votes (6.5%) in elections to the Reichstag. By the December elections of the same year, that figure had fallen to around 907,000 votes (3.0%). Two months after Hitler's release from prison on 27 February, the NSDAP was re-founded and centralised. An index of all members was created and, at the Party conference at **Bamberg** in February 1926, a new autocratic and centralised structure was discussed which stressed complete obedience to Hitler, the **Führerprinzip**, and adherence to the 'Programme of 1920'. This was formally accepted at a membership meeting of the Party in May 1926.

## Legality and reorganisation

From 1924 Hitler insisted that all action had to be dictated by the policy of **'legality'**.
- Instead of violence, legal means would be used to promote the Nazi cause - foremost being to gain seats in elections. This was despite the opposition of some in the Party, such as **Gregor Strasser**, to this policy.
- In the summer of 1926, Captain Franz von Pfeffer was appointed leader of the SA to implement guidelines on the movement's role. From now on the SA was to undertake more mundane roles such as training and the stewarding of rallies.

There were other administrative and organisational reforms undertaken in these years.
- In 1926 the **Hitler Youth** and the **Nazi Students' Association** were founded.
- At the Nuremberg Party Congress in 1927, further reorganisation took place with unsuitable **Gauleiters** (regional party officials) being replaced and the central bureaucracy further reorganised.
- Despite such changes, the performance of the Party in the election of May 1928 was dismal, registering only around 800,000 votes (2.6%) and gaining only 12 seats in the new Reichstag.
- The disappointment at the ballot box acted as a stimulus to further reorganisation and October 1928 saw the creation of the first Nazi professional body, the Association of National Socialist Jurists. This was to be followed in 1929 by similar bodies for doctors, teachers and students.

## Opposition to the Young Plan

Of far greater significance to the fortunes of the Party was the opportunity presented by the campaign against the **Young Plan** from the summer of 1929. The leader of the DNVP, Alfred Hugenburg invited the NSDAP to join the Reich Committee for a Referendum to oppose the Young Plan. The subsequent referendum in December 1929 on the so-called '**Freedom Law**' resulted in humiliation for the coalition, only 13.8% voting in favour. However, the campaign had given Hitler considerable national exposure.

## The Wall Street Crash and the collapse of democracy

- The Wall Street Crash hit German industry hard. The rise in unemployment had an important effect in further polarising German politics.
- In March 1930, the Müller Cabinet broke up after the strains of the coalition became all too apparent over the issue of unemployment insurance.
- The new cabinet was formed on 30 March under the leadership of **Heinrich Brüning** of the Centre Party, but it was heavily influenced by President Hindenberg. Brüning increasingly used Article 48 as the means by which he governed. However, he failed to deal with the worsening economic situation of the time.
- He did, though, end reparations in 1932.
- Hindenberg made it clear that if the government, despite only having minority support in the Reichstag, was brought down by a vote of no confidence he would use Article 48 of the constitution to rule by decree.

## 1930 and the growth in Nazi support

- This period of turmoil in national politics also saw significant changes at local level. In June 1930, the Nazis won 14.4% of the vote in elections for the Saxony **Landtag** (local Parliament), which was over 9% higher than the previous year.
- The result in the September elections to the Reichstag was a triumph for the Nazis. Not only did their representation in the Reichstag increase from 12 to 107 seats, but the vote they achieved increased from 800,000 in 1928 to 6.4 million in 1930.
- As a result of the Nazis' swelling support, the reformed Brüning Cabinet governed with even less support and had to rely on the 'toleration' of the SPD and, ever increasingly, the use of Article 48.

## Growth in Party membership

The election victory of 1930 acted as an important stimulus to Nazi Party membership.

- Between September and the end of the year nearly 100,000 new members joined up and the period saw spectacular growth in sectional party organisations.

- Of particular note was the expansion of the **NS Agararpolititische Apparat** (AA), founded by **Walther Darre** in 1930. Created with the expressed aims of extending Nazi influence in the countryside, developing a vibrant rural organisation and infiltrating existing farmers' organisations, the AA was highly successful.

## Revolt of the SA, 1931

Similar campaign tactics at local level to those used at national level meant that the momentum of election success was maintained. Throughout 1931 the Nazis averaged around 40% in local elections. However the debate over 'legality' within the Party and, in particular, the activities of the SA persisted. In March 1931 the leader of the Berlin SA, **Walther Stennes**, and some of his members rebelled against the orders of Hitler to obey the law. The revolt failed to win the support of the majority of SA troopers, although it highlighted the tensions in the Nazi movement.

## Economic collapse and Nazi opportunity, 1931

It was the economic collapse of the summer of 1931, which again gave the Nazis opportunity and turned attention away from their tactics and divisions. The main aim of Brüning's economic and financial policy had been to remove the burden of reparations. However, in July 1931 there was a banking collapse, followed by financial panic and the closure of all German banks for a 3-week period. The political confusion which followed and the rise in unemployment (which in September stood at 4.3 million) prompted Hugenburg to attempt to re-form a 'National Opposition' of the right with the aim of bringing down Brüning's government. The so-called 'Harzberg Front' of Stahlhelm, DNVP and Nazis met in October 1931 but collapsed after internal arguing.

## Nazi electoral success, 1932

The presidential election of March–April 1932 saw Hindenberg returned to office, but of significance for the future was the vote registered for Hitler. Despite saturation electioneering, the Nazi leader managed to poll only 30.1% on the first ballot and 36.8% on the second, as opposed to Hindenberg's 49.6% and 53%. Yet the Nazis still managed to present such a defeat as a success since their vote had more than doubled from the Reichstag election.

## Political intrigue

An emergency decree of April 1932 banned the SA and SS, mainly in response to growing street violence and evidence that the Nazis had been drawing up plans to stage a coup if Hitler had won the presidential election. This move was taken against a background of intrigue amongst the President's ministers and advisers. The Minister of the Interior, **General Gröner,** who had introduced the ban, was undermined by a whispering campaign led by **General von Schleicher** with the full backing of the Nazis. Schleicher met with Hitler on 8 May 1932. As a result of the meeting, Hitler agreed to accept a new presidential Cabinet in return for the removal of Brüning and the lifting of the ban on the SA and SS.

So now Schleicher could influence the removal of Brüning and help bring about a more right-wing government.

- Gröner resigned from the Cabinet after being shouted down by Nazi deputies in the Reichstag on 10 May.
- Soon after, on 29 May Hindenberg demanded Brüning's resignation, which he received the next day.
- A new cabinet was formed with **Franz von Papen** as Chancellor and Schleicher as the new Minister of Defence.
- The date for new elections to the Reichstag was set for the end of July and the ban on the SA was lifted on 16 June.
- The street violence in the run up to the election left over 100 dead. This violence was used as the perfect excuse for the removal of the SPD-dominated Prussian government, which was overthrown by von Papen on 20 July 1932.
- The SPD failed to react and the unions were weakened by the division on the left between the KPD and SPD.
- The elections to the Reichstag 11 days later saw the Nazis' percentage of the vote increase to 37.3%, which translated into 230 seats making them the largest party in the Reichstag.

## The Nazis are brought to power, 1932–33

- Despite such apparent success, the election did not give the Nazis an outright majority or automatic power and von Papen refused to hand over the Chancellorship to Hitler. As a result, the newly elected Reichstag was immediately dissolved on 12 September 1932, after the government lost a vote of no confidence by 512 votes to 42.
- The new election in November saw a fall in the Nazi vote of some 4% (34 seats) but they were still the largest party. This result simply reinforced the political stalemate.
- Hindenberg wished to continue presidential government but refused to appoint Hitler as Chancellor without his having first achieved a majority in the Reichstag. However, the Nazi leader had the ability (in coalition with the Centre Party) to vote down a government at will. The only perceived alternative for the establishment was to rule without the Reichstag and suppress all opposition.
- In attempting a way out, Hindenberg sacked von Papen and appointed General von Schleicher as Chancellor on 3 December. His first act was to

attempt to draw the Nazis into a coalition by offering the vice-Chancellorship to Gregor Strasser. The leading Nazi's instinct was to accept such an offer as the only way the Party was going to gain power, but he was forced to back down and resign after a fierce battle with Hitler. Without the Nazis, the von Schleicher government lacked support, a fact which soon became apparent with the strong opposition to his economic policy presented on 15 December.

## Hitler's first Cabinet

From 4 January 1933, von Papen and Hitler held talks about the composition of a future government based on a broad nationalist coalition very similar to the Harzberg Front.

- Support for such a coalition came from a variety of sources including the Agrarian League and industrialist organisations. The leading banker **Hjalmar Schacht** supported Hitler and wrote to the President backing his cause. This support had an impact on Hindenberg who turned to von Papen to form a viable government, particularly as it was clear that von Schleicher could command little support in the Reichstag.
- As negotiations between von Papen and Hitler progressed, the former conceded the role of Chancellor to the latter but in a Cabinet that would be a coalition of the right. It was this factor and the acceptability of the prospective Minister of Defence, General von Blomberg, which persuaded Hindenberg to accept von Schleicher's resignation on 27 January and to install Hitler as Chancellor on 30 January.
- The new Cabinet in fact included only three Nazis, Hitler as Chancellor, Wilhelm Frick as Minister for the Interior and Hermann Göring as Minister without Portfolio. The vice-Chancellor was to be Franz von Papen and other parties of the right were well represented, Hugenberg of the DNVP was put in charge of the Economics Ministry and Franz Seldte of the Stadthelm was made Minister of Labour.

# Assessment: The rise of the Nazi Party, 1919–33

## Questions in the style of OCR (Unit 1)

**Q 1a Identify and explain any two reasons for Hitler's appointment as Chancellor in January 1933.** **(30)**

### How to answer this question

The key issue in this question is the Nazis' rise to power. Your answer must focus on an explanation, not on describing what happened or telling the story. To gain top marks, you should explain fully the importance of both factors. Here is a list of factors you might wish to consider when making your choice:
- the intrigue of Hindenberg, von Papen and others
- the economic crisis of 1929-33
- Nazi electoral success 1929-33
- the division of the political opposition.

Once you have identified the two factors that you think are most important you should plan an argument. Here are some examples of arguments which could be used when discussing the influence of the first two factors listed.
- The turning point in the fortunes of the Nazis was the economic depression which followed the Wall Street Crash. This created widespread lack of confidence in the established political system, a situation which the Nazis were able to take advantage of electorally.
- The intrigue of von Papen and others was crucial in Hindenberg's appointment of Hitler as Chancellor. It was the hope of the Reichspresident and others in the establishment that Hitler could be used to restore authoritarian government to Germany.

You must show that you have a good grasp of detail and you must make your points clearly. Here is an extract from a good response to this question.

> Hitler became Chancellor in 1933 because Hindenberg, von Papen and others who had once controlled the Weimar Republic had been undermined and a new more authoritarian regime could be installed peacefully. This could only take place if it had a base of popular support – which only the Nazis on the right of the political spectrum could provide. The poor judgement of von Papen and Hindenberg in believing that they could control and use the Nazi movement is crucial in explaining the Nazi seizure of power.

From 1930 onwards, government was conducted by intrigue and deals, e.g. the removal of Gröner and Brüning from office in May 1932. As a reaction to Schleicher's economic policy of late 1932 which was seen as far too conciliatory to the left, initiatives were undertaken to create a government of the right which included the NSDAP. These initiatives were centred around von Papen who resented his treatment at the hands of von Schleicher the previous year. Yet he was not acting alone: there were members of the business community, e.g. Kurt von Schröder, who disliked von Schleicher's reforms of September 1932 and were determined to see a return to a more authoritarian rule, whether it be under the Chancellorship of von Papen or Hitler. Through their intrigue, Hindenberg was convinced of Hitler's suitability for the post of Chancellor.

Q  **b How important a reason for Nazi electoral success in the years 1929–32 was the economic depression in Germany that followed the Wall Street Crash?** **(60)**

## How to answer this question

This question focuses on the years 1929-32. However you should use background information when considering long term factors. First you must consider the impact of the rapid increase in unemployment and the collapse in economic confidence on the voting intentions of Germans. However, this question asks you to focus on 'how important?' The answer to this is that the depression was important but there are other factors to be considered.

Here is an extract from a candidate's response to this question.

The Nazis very much benefited from the discontent produced by the rapid rise in unemployment during late 1929 and 1930. The Nazis presented themselves as a party of discontent and therefore were a natural political home for some of Germany's six million unemployed in 1932 (although many voted for the KPD). The banking crisis in 1931 was a turning point for many of the middle class who saw their savings swallowed up in the financial chaos. It was this section of society that formed the bedrock of support for the Nazis. The election of July 1932 saw the Nazis receive 37.3 per cent of the votes in the elections for the Reichstag which gave them 230 seats.

However, it was not only the depression that is to blame for the growth in the Nazi electoral success. The Nazi party reforms of the 1920s meant that it was able to take advantage of the political chaos in the years 1930-32. The agricultural wing, the AA (founded in 1930) attracted a discontented peasantry to the party. The Nazis were a national organisation and, as such, had officials and officers in most regions. The tactics of identifying and targeting groups in certain regions brought electoral success; in local elections in Saxony in 1929 the Nazis achieved 14.4 per cent of the votes which was a large improvement on the figure in the national election of 1929.

## Question in the style of Edexel (Unit 1)

Study Sources A to E and then answer questions 1–5.

**Source A** Adapted from the first Nazi programme, Munich, 24 February 1920.

2 We demand equal status for Germany compared to other nations and the ending of the Peace Treaties drawn up at Versailles and St Germain.

7 We demand that the first priority of the state should be to ensure that its citizens have a job and a decent life.

16 We demand the establishment and maintenance of a healthy middle class. The large department stores should be placed under the control of the local authority and should be rented out to small businesses at low prices. All small businesses should have the keenest regard for their deliveries to the state, the Länder or the local authorities.

**Source B** Adapted from *Knaves, Fools and Heroes in Europe between the Wars*, by J. Wheeler-Bennet, 1974. Wheeler-Bennet was an Englishman who lived in Germany in the early 1930s.

There were many who, for the moment were ready to give their support to the new government. It must be remembered that in the course of the fifteen years which separated the day Hitler was made Chancellor from the Armistice of 1918 Germany had experienced governments of every kind of political combination and complexion, had suffered terrifying bankruptcy and had failed to obtain any revision of the Treaty of Versailles. These people genuinely believed that economic breakdown, a paralysing inflation and a Communist takeover were possible, probable and imminent. On these fears Hitler had based his popular appeal. He had something for everyone in his bag of promises, and above all he offered an alternative.

How to Pass AS Modern World History

**Source C** From *Years of Weimar and the Third Reich*, by David Evans and Jane Jenkins, 1999.

> Hitler presented himself as a man of the people who would save Germany from decline. Propaganda reinforced this image. Hitler promised that he would heal all class rifts and better conflicts, that he would weld society together for the greater good. The message was simple – vote Nazi for a reborn Germany. The context of the early 1930s, with 8.5 million unemployed people, favoured Hitler. There was a feeling that Germany needed a strong leader. The Nazis staged political rallies which combined with Hitler's speeches captured the imagination of the masses.
>
> A study of the percentages of votes cast in the different electoral districts of Germany shows the significance of religion and industrialisation in determining [Nazi] support. The height of Nazi electoral popularity in 'free' elections, which came in July 1932, provides a clear picture of this. Catholic voters of all classes remained loyal to the Centre Party, as did the working classes to the SDP. This would suggest that support for the Nazis came from the Protestant middle class.

**Q 1** **Study Source A. Using the source explain why some groups/classes supported the Nazis.**

**How to answer this question**

The question is asking you to show that you understand the source. Therefore you must do the following:
- Provide some explanation which answers the question.
- Extract brief quotes from the source to back up what you are saying.

**Style** Below is an extract from a candidate's answer to this question:

> The source shows how the Nazis attempted to appeal to those groups in German society that felt threatened or discontented. The Nazis won the support of many of the *Mittelstand* who felt threatened by economic change, especially with their promise to take over department stores and have them 'rented out to small businesses at low prices'.

**Q 2** **Using your own knowledge, explain what is meant by the term 'revolutionary' in the context of Nazism.**

**How to answer this question**

The question asks you to show your understanding of Nazi ideology and beliefs. You need to respond with a thorough examination of the Twenty Point programme of 1920, Hitler's promises and the events of 1923.

**Q 3** Study Sources B and C and refer to both sources in your answer to this question: 'The Nazis were a party of protest.' To what extent do you agree with this statement?

## How to answer this question

You need to look for examples in the sources of the Nazis being a party of protest. The question asks you to use the sources and you need to focus on what they say in your answer.

**Plan** Before you write you need to come to some kind of conclusion about how you will answer the question. An example might be along the lines of the following:
'This statement is generally convincing. There are examples in both sources that agree with the statement.'
You should also underline in the source examples of change and of continuity.

**Style** Make sure that you quote from the sources when making your point. Below is an example of the style you might adopt in answering this question.

> In 1933 the priority for many Germans was the restoration of economic stability because, as Source B states, Germany 'had suffered terrifying bankruptcy'. The appeal of the Nazis was to those who wished to protest at the economic chaos of the period and those who feared that this chaos would soon engulf them. Source C puts this very clearly stating that 'Hitler presented himself as a man of the people who would save Germany from decline'.

**Q 4** Study Sources B and C. How useful are these Sources to an historian studying the reasons why some Germans supported the Nazis in the 1920s and early 1930s?

## How to answer this question

When answering a question about the value of a source you should try to avoid generalisations about the type of source and you should concentrate on more than its content. Instead you should ask yourself the questions listed on page 11.

**Q 5** Using any two of the sources and your own knowledge, do you agree that Hitler was made chancellor in 1933 because of the strengths of the Nazi Party?

How to Pass AS Modern World History

## How to answer this question

This question asks you to analyse the reasons why Hitler was made Chancellor in 1933. To reach full marks you will need to do the following:
- Look for a variety of reasons to explain why Hitler was offered the Chancellorship
- Prioritise your most important reasons
- Use information from both the sources and your own knowledge
- Plan your line of argument first and what you are going to put in each paragraph.

**Plan** You might use these points of argument in your plan.
- The Nazis were the preferred option for an establishment that hoped to use Hitler to create a more authoritarian type of government.
- Hindenberg was persuaded to appoint Hitler as Chancellor as he and his movement were fiercely anti-communist.
- The Nazis were well organised and a mass movement. They used new and powerful propaganda techniques, were ideologically flexibility and seemed prepared to work with the establishment.
- Their appeal was reinforced by the apparent 'legality' of the Nazi assault on power in the late 1920s and early 30s in contrast to the attempted putsch of 1923.

# Section 4: German foreign policy and the road to war

## Hitler's foreign policy objectives

Throughout his political career, Hitler's foreign policy objectives remained constant and clear. They were clearly expressed in Mein Kampf and numerous articles and speeches. Hitler believed in the following.

- **Versailles** Hitler despised the Treaty of Versailles and saw it as a national humiliation. He promised that if he came to power he would tear up the Treaty, end Germany's reparation payments to the Allies and restore Germany's borders to where they had been in 1914.
- **Lebensraum** In Mein Kampf and elsewhere he argued that the Aryan race demanded lebensraum (living space) in the east. This living space would be in what is now Poland and Russia.
- **Nationalism** Hitler was a nationalist who believed that Germany should be respected diplomatically. He also strongly believed in the union of German-speaking peoples. This would include a union between Germany and Austria, the country of his birth.
- **Anti-communism** He hated communism and promised the destruction of that ideology world-wide if he came to power.
- **Economic expansion** Hitler's economic policy of rearmament meant that Germany needed raw materials such as coal, iron ore and oil. It also needed to increase its industrial capacity. Therefore, Hitler's foreign policy aims were geared to ensuring a guaranteed supply of materials.

## 1933

Within a year of his appointment as Chancellor, Hitler had withdrawn Germany from the Disarmament Conference and the League of Nations. From the start, the regime took very little note of international convention or agreements. The League of Nations had been weakened by the actions of Japan in Manchuria in 1931–32. By leaving the League, Hitler made it clear that Germany would have to be dealt with by individual members of the world community. However, Hitler needed to avoid any foreign conflict until the regime was secure at home. In 1934 he signed a 10-year **Non-Aggression Pact** with Poland which ensured the security of Germany's eastern borders. Of particular importance was the fact that this treaty broke the French system of alliances in eastern Europe.

## The Austria Crisis of 1934

- The Treaty of Versailles had banned political union between Germany and Austria. However, such a union was one of Hitler's cherished ambitions. From 1933, Hitler backed a campaign by Austrian Nazis to undermine the government of that country led by Engelbert Dollfuss. Their actions

How to Pass AS Modern World History

included blowing up strategically important buildings and attacking important government officials.

- On 25 July 1934 Austrian Nazis murdered Dollfuss. However their attempt to take power was foiled by government troops led by **Dr Kurt von Schuschnigg**. The affair raised the possibility of Nazi intervention in Austria.
- This was made impossible by the actions of Benito Mussolini who deployed 40,000 troops along the Austrian border. Italy's northern borders are shared with Austria, amongst others. The Italian leader did not relish the possibility of German troops on Italy's northern borders and acted fast to deter Hitler from making any move. Mussolini twice received visits from Dr von Schuschnigg in the autumn of 1934 to confirm his support for Austrian independence.

## The Saar, 1935

As stated above, Hitler's aim was to destroy the Versailles Treaty and to restore to Germany what he believed was rightfully hers.

- In January 1935 a plebiscite (vote) was held in the **Saarland** over whether the region should return to German control, stay under League of Nations' jurisdiction or be transferred to French control.
- The vote was legitimate under the terms of the Treaty of Versailles and was carried out by the League of Nations. The Nazis campaigned for a vote to join Germany. The electors of the region responded with a 90% yes vote to join Germany.
- On March 1 the Saarland was formally reabsorbed into the German Reich. Up until this point, Hitler had been wary of upsetting Britain and France. However, with the plebiscite won, it opened the possibility of further territorial gain.

## Rearmament and conscription, 1935

- The Versailles Treaty had limited the size of the Wehrmacht as well as Germany's Navy and Air Force. In March 1935, Hitler announced that Germany formally renounced the sections of the Treaty of Versailles concerned with her disarmament.
- Immediately he reintroduced conscription and rearmament. The Wehrmacht was to be increased in size to 36 divisions. Hitler justified his actions by arguing that both France and the Soviet Union were increasing the size of their armed forces against the spirit of Versailles.
- France reacted strongly to German rearmament and encouraged Britain and Italy to protest. The three countries met at the **Stresa Conference** in April 1935. The conference was called with the aim of establishing a common front against Germany. However, the signing of the Anglo-German Naval Agreement (see over) undermined this common front.
- In April 1935 the League of Nations criticised Germany's rejection of

Versailles. However, Hitler saw that there was not a solid alliance formed against Germany. Britain was interested in protecting her Empire and in June 1935 signed a separate Anglo-German Naval Agreement with Germany. This allowed Germany a Navy which was 35% of the size of the British fleet. It was the willingness of the allies to deal separately with Germany that allowed Hitler to expand unchecked.

## Anti-communism and the Spanish Civil War, 1936–39

- Hitler's involvement in the Spanish Civil War was crucial to the eventual victory of **General Franco's** nationalists. He was determined to help defeat what he saw as a communist Republic.
- Hitler used the war as a training ground for troops and a testing ground for new technology.
- Germany's involvement in Spain was part of Hitler's commitment to fight what he saw as the spread of communism. A further example of this commitment was the signing of the Anti-Comitern Pact with Japan in November 1937. However, this treaty was also an extension of the **German–Italian Axis** formed in October 1936.

## Rhineland, 1936

One of Hitler's most dangerous political gambles was the remilitarisation of the Rhineland in March 1936. The **Wehrmacht** (army) was not of any great strength and would not have been able to resist French intervention. However, Hitler was prepared to take the risk and ordered German troops into the region. This was another violation of Versailles and a challenge to the French. However, the French did not respond militarily. The diplomatic world was distracted by the Ethiopian crisis and Britain was not prepared to introduce sanctions against Germany.

## Danzig, 1933–39

One of Hitler's most common criticisms of the Treaty of Versailles was the creation of the Polish Corridor and the provision for the League of Nations to control the port of Danzig.
- In 1933, the Nazis in Danzig won 39 seats out of 72 in the Senate that ran the port. Two years later in 1935 they won 43 seats.
- Encouraged by Hitler, the Danzig Nazis slowly undermined their opponents and, as the influence of the League of Nations declined, so their ability to restrain the Danzig Nazis disappeared.
- By 1938, 70 seats in the Senate were held by Nazis, laws against Jews had been passed and, to all intents and purposes, the city had become part of the German Reich. These measures show the extent that Hitler and his Party were prepared to go in destroying Versailles.

## Ethiopia Crisis, 1935–36

In 1935 the Italian dictator Benito Mussolini ordered the invasion of

How to Pass AS Modern World History

Ethiopia in Africa. The League of Nations condemned Mussolini's actions and imposed limited sanctions on the Italy. The **German–Italian axis** was formed in 1936 as a result of the Ethiopian crisis. In response to British and French criticism of his action in Africa, Mussolini concluded that an alliance with her ideological partner Nazi Germany was more suitable. The axis of 1936 resulted in the military alliance, the **Pact of Steel** signed in May 1939.

## Anschluss, 1938

- In March 1938, Hitler fulfilled a long-cherished personal ambition by invading Austria and proclaiming **Anschluss** (union) between Germany and Austria.
- Mussolini's opposition was reduced by Italy's involvement in the Spanish Civil War (see below) and his desire to develop the strong alliance with Germany that had begun in 1936. Therefore, when Schuschnigg visited Italy in 1937, Mussolini informed him that Austria could not rely on Italian support in a war against Germany.
- Hitler continued to pressurise the Austrian government. In February 1938, von Schuschingg visited Hitler and agreed to an amnesty for Austrian Nazis in prison.
- Internal chaos and pressure from the Nazis resulted in an ultimatum presented to the Austrian government in March 1939. The Nazi Arthur Seyss-Inquart seized the chancellorship and German troops invaded on 12 March.
- A plebiscite on Anschluss was held in Austria in April 1938 with a 99.75% 'yes' vote. Again British and French protests at the undermining of Versailles were half hearted. Hitler had managed to destroy Versailles whilst the leading democracies continued to believe that a policy of appeasement was the only way to deal with the successive crises.

## Czechoslovakia, 1938

After Anschluss with Austria, Hitler turned his attention to Czechoslovakia.
- Before 1919 the provinces which made up Czechoslovakia were part of the Austro-Hungarian Empire. Therefore, there was a considerable German-speaking minority in Czechoslovakia called the Sudeten Germans. Hitler believed that these 3.5 million Sudeten Germans, who were concentrated near the borders with Germany and Austria, should become part of the German Reich.
- Czechoslovakia was also attractive for Germany in other ways, it was rich in raw materials and the **Skoda** engineering company was one of the largest in Europe.
- In February 1938, Hitler promised protection to German minorities outside the Reich's borders. This was a clear signal that he was preparing to interfere in the affairs of Czechoslovakia.
- The Anschluss with Austria in March 1938 completely changed the

situation as the new German Empire surrounded Czechoslovakia on three sides.

- In April 1938, the Sudeten German leader Konrad Henlein presented a series of demands to the Czechoslovak government led by Dr Milan Hodza. Known as the **Karlsbad Programme**, the demands were entirely unacceptable and immediately rejected. This was despite encouragement from Czechoslovakia's allies Britain and France that they should accept.
- The Karlsbad Programme included full autonomy for predominately Sudeten regions, reparations for any damages suffered by Germans since 1918, a revision of Czech foreign policy and full cultural freedom.
- Throughout the summer negotiations continued between the government and Sudeten leaders. As tension rose all major powers put their armed forces on alert; in September 1938 Britain held naval manoeuvres and France called up her reserves.
- On 12 September Hitler increased the tension by demanding self-determination for the Sudeten Germans. In September he twice met with the British Prime Minister Neville Chamberlain at Berchtesgaden and Godesberg. Hitler demanded that Czechoslovakia surrender the predominantly Sudeten territories and that there should be plebiscites held in areas with large Sudeten minorities by November.
- Britain and France both wished to appease Germany but Chamberlain and the French Prime Minister Daladier found these proposals unacceptable. Eventually Hitler was persuaded by Mussolini to hold an international conference on the issue.

### The Munich Conference, September 1938

The conference was held to resolve the Czechoslovakia crisis. Whilst Britain, Italy, France and Germany were represented, Czechoslovakia was not. The agreement that was signed at Munich represented a considerable diplomatic victory for Hitler. Although some in Britain and France protested against the destruction of the last democratic country in central Europe, there was considerable relief in those countries that war had been avoided.

- German occupation of mainly Sudeten areas was to take place at the beginning of October 1938.
- In all Germany gained 10,000 square miles containing 3.5 million inhabitants of which 700,000 were Czechs.

### Appeasement

It was at Munich that the British and French policy of appeasement was most clearly seen. The policy is most commonly associated with the British Prime Minister Neville Chamberlain. However the roots of appeasement are far more complex. Britain and France suffered horrendously in the First World War and, in the 1930s, their foreign policy priorities still lay in the Empire. A more aggressive anti-German stance would not have been supported by the isolationist USA or the self-absorbed USSR. Britain did not have the financial resources to rearm sufficiently rapidly to fight a full scale war against Germany. However, in 1935 she did start rearmament but it was more gradual.

## The annexation of the remains of Czechoslovakia, March 1939

Hitler's ambitions for territory beyond the limits of Versailles' provisions and Germany's racial borders became apparent in March 1939. On 15 March the Czech provinces of Bohemia and Moravia became German provinces, to be followed the next day by Slovakia. More than any other action, the destruction of Czechoslovakia proved to the outside world that Hitler's ambition lay in achieving lebensraum.

Hitler did not stop there. In the same month he put pressure on Lithuania to give up Memel and made demands regarding the Polish Corridor. In response to such aggression, Britain and France promised help to Poland in March 1939 if she was invaded by Hitler.

### Nazi–Soviet Pact, 1939

Throughout the 1930s, Hitler's foreign policy had been fiercely anti-communist. This was seen in Germany's involvement in the Spanish Civil War between 1936–39. However, in August 1939, Hitler sent his foreign Minister von Ribbentrop to Moscow to sign a non-aggression pact with the Soviet Union. Such a move was greeted with amazement across the diplomatic world. The main points of the pact ensured that Germany could attack Poland without provoking a response from the Soviet Union. On August 31, 1939 the Supreme Soviet of the Soviet Union finally agreed the terms of the treaty. The following day Hitler invaded Poland.

# Assessment: German foreign policy and the road to war

## Questions in the style of OCR (Unit 3)

**Q 1a** **Identify and explain any two reasons for the outbreak of war in 1939.** **(30)**

### How to answer this question

You must first identify a list of reasons for the outbreak of war. Here is a list of examples:

- German territorial ambitions
- the policy of appeasement
- economic problems
- the Treaty of Versailles.

To be awarded a high mark for your answer to this question you need to:

- explain any two reasons for the war in detail
- link the factors directly to the outbreak of war.

In this extract the candidate attempts to link the issue of the Treaty of Versailles directly to the outbreak of war.

> Hitler's destruction of the Treaty of Versailles was at the root of his ideology. It also was of primary importance politically – he had come to power promising to destroy Versailles. Hitler was obsessed with Versailles. He saw its destruction, e.g. anschluss in 1938, as the means by which Germany could dominate central and eastern Europe. However Hitler's commitment to the destruction of the Treaty was a direct cause of war because in being so committed he threatened limitless German expansion in Europe. In response to his demands made to the Polish government about the Polish Corridor (which had been removed from German control at Versailles), Britain and France signed a pact of assistance in April 1939. It was this pact that led to war being declared in September 1939.

**Q 1b** **To what extent did Hitler bring about change in German foreign policy from 1933–39?** **(60)**

### How to answer this question

You should examine the various means by which Hitler changed German foreign policy. The question asks you to look at the 'extent' to which Hitler brought about change. The answer is that he brought about change to a considerable extent. The features of change might include:

How to Pass AS Modern World History

- destruction of the Treaty of Versailles
- expansionist foreign policy
- support for anti-democratic movements abroad, e.g. Franco's nationalists.

Answers in the top bands will explain the extent of change but will also recognise the limits of change. In particular you should try and point out that, until 1938, Hitler was attempting to restore Germany's 1914 borders. There were signs before 1938, however, of Hitler's contempt for international opinion.

### Further question in the style of OCR (Unit 3)

Q  1a  **Explain Hitler's foreign policy aims after 1933.** (30)
   b  **Compare the responsibility of Germany, Britain and France for the failure to avoid war in 1939.** (60)

# Section 5: German economic policy, 1933–45

## Work schemes and the reduction in unemployment

The most important challenge facing the Nazis on taking office was to reduce unemployment. Within the first year, legislation and initiatives were introduced which dealt effectively with the number of Germans out of work. **The Law to Reduce Unemployment** of June 1933 increased the number of **Arbeitdeinst** (work schemes). This was part of an overall job creation plan which included the building of new roads, the autobahnen. The so-called 'Battle for Work' was extended by the government which lent money to private companies so as they could create jobs.

## State investment

State investment totalling 5 billion Reichsmarks was poured into work creation schemes between 1932–35.
- In June 1933, the first law was passed releasing money to build the first autobahn.
- The Labour Service and Emergency Relief Schemes, which put thousands back to work, were labour intensive.
- The regime's attempts to reduce unemployment were successful. In 1933 the percentage of the workforce which was unemployed was 25.9%. This figure had fallen to 7.4% by 1936.

## Hjalmar Schacht and the New Plan

- In May 1933, Hitler appointed Hjalmar Schacht as President of the Reichsbank. One of Schacht's first acts was to increase state control of foreign trade.
- In the summer of 1934 Schacht was made Minister of Economics. He promptly introduced the 'New Plan' in September 1934 which gave the government extensive powers to regulate trade and currency transactions. This **'New Plan'** was introduced in the face of a foreign exchange crisis (which was the result of Germany importing more goods than it exported). The aim of the 'New Plan' was to make Germany independent of the world trading system.
- In 1934 Schacht also proceeded to negotiate a series of trade agreements with countries in South America and south east Europe. The aim of these was to prevent Germany running up a huge foreign currency deficit, whilst still being able to procure essential raw materials.
- Schacht also created the policy which was aimed at encouraging a growth in demand in the economy. This was done with the introduction of **Mefo Bills**. These were bills issued by the government as payment for goods. They were then held by investors or banks and could either be exchanged for cash or held for up to 5 years, earning 4% interest a year.

How to Pass AS Modern World History

## 1936–39, Guns versus butter?

- Hitler's main long-term objective was to create an economy which could support sustained rearmament. By 1936 the economy had recovered to such an extent as to make such a move possible. However, there were problems which potentially could prevent this happening.
- By 1935, Germany was still importing large amounts of foodstuffs such as butter and vegetable oil. The 'Production Battle' began in 1934 with the aim of increasing the production of foodstuffs in Germany. However, this was not so easily done.
- Agriculture suffered from a lack of machinery and, increasingly, manpower. The head of the Reich Food Estate, Walther Darré asked Schacht for foreign currency to import food, with the alternative being the introduction of rationing. However, Germany also needed to import raw materials such as lead and copper to sustain rearmament.
- The crisis grew worse by 1936 as Germany used up her reserves of raw materials and was now forced to buy raw materials such as oil, on the open market for cash. The problem facing Schacht was the fact that Germany could not afford to import large quantities of food **and** raw materials for rearmament. The only politically acceptable answer to this problem was to cut imports and embark on a policy of greater self-sufficiency.

## The Second Four Year Plan, 1936–40

In April 1936, Hermann Göring was appointed Commissioner of Raw Materials, giving him responsibility for making the German economy self-sufficient. This was to be partly achieved by synthetically manufacturing rubber and oil. Göring's influence extended to control over the Second Four Year Plan, which was based on the policy of **autarky** (self-sufficiency). Göring set up a separate organisation for the Four Year Plan which was to become the most important of the departments concerned with the economy. Worried by the pace of rearmament and bitter at his loss of influence, Schacht resigned as Minister of Economics in November 1937 to be replaced by Walther Funk. From this moment on, Göring took full control of the economy. Targets were set by Göring for the increased production of oil, rubber and steel. The construction of the huge **Reichswerke Hermann Göring** at Watenstadt-Salzgitter was testament to the drive to produce essential war goods in Germany. In 1937–38, money spent on the military rose to 10 billion marks and by 1938–39 this figure had risen to 17 billion marks.

## The limitations of autarky

The policy of self-sufficiency was not a complete success. By 1938 Germany's balance of trade deficit had risen to 432 million Reichsmarks.

One reason was that the regime did not want to squeeze the consumer too much – the Nazis had come to power partly as a result of economic depression. Hitler, in particular, was acutely aware of how unpopular the regime might become if basic consumer goods were unavailable. Therefore, although consumer spending power did not rise significantly from 1936–39, neither did it decline.

## Organisation of the war economy

The idea of a Blitzkreig war economy supposes that Hitler and his generals planned a series of short wars. The reason that this strategy was adopted was that Germany lacked sufficient raw materials to fight a wider war of conquest. Such materials, therefore, could only be acquired through short, rapid conquests.

The outbreak of war in September 1939 saw confusion in the planning of the German war effort. In March 1940, however a Ministry of Munitions was created under Fritz Todt which went some way to coordinating this area of production. The invasion of the Soviet Union in 1941, the failure of the Blitzkreig military campaign and the prospect of a prolonged struggle on the eastern front led to the rethinking of economic policy.

## Rationalisation and the appointment of Speer

On 3 December 1941, Hitler issued the **Führer Order** on the **'Simplification and Increased Efficiency in Armaments Production'** which demanded that Todt rationalise the armaments industry. Thereafter, there was a significant change in priorities.
- Industry accepted responsibility for raising levels of production with central direction coming from Todt's ministry.
- In February 1942, Albert Speer was appointed as Todt's successor in the post of Minister for Weapons and Munitions. Speer was to develop Todt's plans for rationalisation of industry and the more efficient control of raw material distribution.

## Raw material and labour shortages, 1939–41

The economy was hampered by a shortage of labour, which became apparent in the early days of the war.
- By May 1940 there were 3.5 million less workers in the workforce than one year before. The situation was made worse by 1.7 million workers being drafted into the armed forces in 1941, and a further 1.4 million were called up between May 1941 and May 1942.
- As a result, the Nazis resorted to recruiting foreign labour and by the end of 1942 there were some 6.4 million foreign workers in Germany.
- Despite a reluctance to conscript women, the pressures on the economy led to a gradual rethink. In January 1943, women between the ages of

17 and 45 were obliged to sign up for work, although out of this only some 400,000 were finally recruited.

- From 1943 to the end of the war, 2.5 million extra foreign workers were employed in often brutal conditions.

## Raw materials

Germany lacked the natural resources – iron, coal, oil and other materials – needed for a sustained war effort. It was this factor that, more than any other, shaped Nazi war aims and plans.

- German access to **oil** was limited, the main supplier being Romania, which exported nearly 3 million tons to her ally in 1943. However, this was not enough to supply an economy and armed forces which from 1942 were engaged in Total War.
- Even conquest did not ensure an increased supply of needed materials. Despite the increase in available iron ore and the acquisition of the steel industries of the Low Countries and France, there was a chronic shortage of steel throughout the war and particularly before 1942. In 1941 it was calculated that demand for steel exceeded supply by 30%.
- This was mostly due to a shortage of coal, despite Germany's large natural reserves and the acquisition of large mining reserves in the Soviet Union and Belgium. As with other industries, however, the Soviets destroyed virtually all they had to leave behind.
- The failure of the Nazis to exploit fully the raw materials of the countries they occupied was crucial in preventing the expansion of the German economy necessary to fight a major war.

## The move to Total War

In February 1943 Göbbels' speech at the Berlin Sportsplatz, in which he called for universal labour service and the closure of all nonessential business, marked a shift to Total War. Such a move to improve production and productivity was reinforced by the appointment of Speer as Reich Minister for Armaments and Production in September 1943. This post gave Speer responsibility for all industrial output and raw materials and he reorganised and rationalised these areas, introducing the **Armaments Commission** in 1943. This was set up to improve the co-operation and co-ordination between the design and manufacturing processes in munitions.

The economy became more productive as the war continued, despite the ever greater numbers of forced labourers. The Armaments Commission created by Speer worked to standardise production, thereby allowing greater mass production. The achievements were impressive:

- In 1944 the number of tank models was reduced from 18 to 7 and types of different vehicles cames down from 55 to 14. The result was a greater productivity which was missing from the Blitzkreig economy.
- In the arms industry, output per head fell from 1939–40 by 12.5%,

mainly because of the effects of conscription and the concentration on consumer industries, which in the same period saw output increase by nearly 16%. However, central control of raw materials, the reduction of hand-working practices and more realistic contracts then produced a rise in output per head in armaments, so by 1943 the figure was 32% higher than that in 1939.

- Better processes cut the amount of precious raw materials used, e.g. for each gun there was a reduction of 93% in the aluminium used after rationalisation had taken place.
- During the last years of the war there was a significant improvement in industrial production, despite Allied bombing. An example of this phenomenon was the BMW engine for planes – the production of which increased by 200% between 1941–43 with an increase of only 12% in the workforce.
- Another impressive example was the use of production line assembly in the manufacturing of the Panzer III tank in 1943, which cut by 50% the time taken for its assembly.
- In the manufacture of munitions, output per worker rose by 60% from 1939–44, again despite the disruption caused by Allied bombing.

## The working class during the war years

The regime was successful in sustaining working-class morale during the first 3 years of the war. This was largely due to the spectacular successes of the German Army until 1941. It was also due to the fact that the workers suffered relatively little material hardship. Fear of working-class opposition forced the regime to adopt a wage freeze in September 1939 rather than making wage cuts. Night work and holiday bonuses were quickly restored after workers responded to their abolition with absenteeism. The system of food and clothing rationing was accepted with little opposition from workers. The system avoided the injustices and **profiteering** of the First World War and was relatively generous. However, working-class morale declined significantly following the winter of 1941–42.

## The battle to keep morale high, 1942–45

The failure to defeat the Soviet Union and the declaration of war on the United States in December 1941 alarmed public opinion. There was growing exhaustion and increasing criticism of state propaganda. But Allied air raids from the spring of 1942 helped to generate a degree of popular solidarity and bolstered the determination to **'stick it out' (aushausen)**. The propaganda minister **Joseph Göbbels** was particularly effective in raising working-class morale by visiting bombed out towns, such as Dortmund which was destroyed in May 1943 and Hamburg which was heavily bombed in July 1943. Nonetheless, not even his spectacular **'Total War speech'** in February 1943 could disguise the problems facing Germany after the disaster of Stalingrad. By 1944 the shortage of supplies and the growing sense that distribution of goods was becoming more unfair led to a swelling black market. However, despite all these problems and the collapse in morale, there was hostility to the assassination attempt on Hitler's life in July 1944.

## Göbbels' and Speer's influence increases, 1944

In 1944 the war deteriorated considerably for the Nazis on all fronts. In July an attempted assassination plot against Hitler resulted in the appointment of the trusted Göbbels to the post of Reich Plenipotentiary for Total War. This gave Göbbels even greater control over production and allowed Speer more scope for change. This was because, in the permanent infighting that characterised the Nazi state, Speer was a close ally of Göbbels.

## The economy collapses, 1945

As the Allies crossed the borders of Germany in early 1945, Hitler's demands for a policy of **'scorched earth'** and the destruction of all industry, was resisted by Speer. It was apparent that defeat was inevitable and Hitler ordered the evacuation of all in the path of the advancing armies. From January 1945 the German economy was in a state of collapse, partly as a consequence of invasion but also due to exhaustion and the effects of the Allied bombing programme. Indeed the bombing campaign had reduced production of essential war materials by anything up to 40% in 1944.

# Assessment: German economic policy, 1933–45

## Questions in the style of Edexcel (Unit 3)

Read Source A and answer the questions that follow.

**Source A** From *Weimar and Nazi Germany 1919–1945*, by M Collier and P Pedley, 2000.

> The introduction of the Four Year Plan marked a turning point in the Nazi regime's economic policy. There was a change in emphasis to an increase in investment in military expenditure. In 1936, 9.4 per cent of Net Domestic Product was invested in armaments. By 1939 that figure had risen to 38.1 per cent. Despite this decisive shift in priorities, there was not a radical restructuring of the economy. Indeed, the period should be seen as a further step on the road to a war economy but with an understanding that autarky was by no means complete. There were significant failures to make Germany self-sufficient by 1939, e.g. on the eve of war Germany was only producing 18 per cent of the demanded amount of synthetic oil. In this sense the nature of economic change very much matched that of the regime. Whilst its intentions were crystal clear, other economic considerations still had to be taken into account.

**Q 1a  How do the authors of this source judge the achievements of the Four Year Plan? Explain your answer.**                                    **(5)**

### How to answer this question

Your task is to show that you understand how the authors of the source reached their interpretation of events.

- By asking you to explain your answer, the question is also directing you to explain the authors' view of the Four Year Plan using your own knowledge.
- You should quote from the source where possible. However, you should ensure that your quotes are short and to the point.

You must answer questions like this directly. Here is an example of an extract from an answer showing how you might do this.

> The authors of this source qualify the extent to which the Four Year Plan reached its stated aims. Despite the aim of self-sufficiency there were considerable disappointments and as the authors write 'autarky was by no means complete'. One of the problems for the regime was that, despite

Q   b  **What were the priorities of Nazi economic policy in the years 1933–39?**                                                                    (7)

**How to answer this question**

Although there is a source at the start of the exercise, this question does not ask you to use it if you do not want to. Instead, the source can act as a stimulus; it can give you a clue to at least a part of your answer. In this case it mentions rearmament, which was one of the main aims of Nazi economic policy.

This question asks you to describe the priorities of Nazi economic policy. It would be a good idea to organise your description thematically. Themes you might include are:
• rearmament, autarky, reduction of unemployment, and maintenance of living standards.

Q   c  **How did Nazi economic policy affect the German people in the period 1933–39?**                                                              (15)

**How to answer this question**

To answer this question you are to use the source, but again only as a stimulus. The question asks for an analytical answer. Therefore, you must:
• answer with a strong line of argument and make a clear judgement, coming down on one or other side of the question
• show you understand that different groups in society were affected in different ways
• use well-selected evidence to back up your argument.

### Questions in the style of OCR (Unit 3)

Q   2a **Identify and explain any two problems that slowed-up the Nazi war effort between 1939 and 1945.**                                           (30)

**How to answer this question**

The question asks you to show that you understand the main features of the German war economy. It also asks you to explain the importance of the two factors you choose. Here is a list of problems:
• Labour shortages
• Partial mobilisation of the economy

- Lack of raw materials
- Allied bombing.

Here is an example of part of a good answer to the question, focussing on the problem of labour shortages.

> An obvious problem for Germany was the labour shortfall, made worse by the demands of the military which was 9.5 million strong by 1943. There had also been losses of 1.7 million up to this point – people who had also been taken out of the labour market. The only answer was the use of foreign labour. By 1944 35 per cent of armaments workers were from abroad and, in total, as many as 9 or 10 million were employed. There was no alternative to the use of foreign labour given the constraints in supply of domestic labour. Yet foreign labour was comparatively unproductive and generally unwilling. This is not surprising considering the appalling conditions in which many workers were kept.

**Q  b  Compare the importance of at least three factors that influenced Nazi economic policy between 1939 and 1945.**          **(60)**

## How to answer this question

To answer this question you need to show the links between the factors you have chosen. You must also prioritise the importance of those factors.

Here is an example of the style which you might use when answering this question.

> One of the most significant factors which shaped Nazi economic policy was her lack of resources. Germany lacked natural resources – iron, coal, oil and the other materials it needed for a sustained war effort. It was this factor which, more than any other, shaped Nazi war aims and plans. A clear example is that of iron ore. Germany lacked high grade iron ore. In order to compensate, the Reichswerke Hermann Göring attempted to develop the production of low grade ore for manufacturing purposes. Yet this could never meet growing military demands, thereby making Germany part-dependent on mostly Swedish imports. During the war the amount of ore imported from neutral Sweden remained practically constant – in 1940 it was 5.4 million tons; in 1943 it was 5.6 million tons. However, the annexations of Austria, Bohemia, Poland and Alsace Lorraine by 1940 brought with them huge quantities of high quality iron ore. In 1943 these areas alone produced 6.7 million tons for the Nazi war effort. Despite this increase, the raw material potential from the occupied countries was only ever partially mobilised.

## Further question in the style of OCR (Unit 3)

Q   3a   Explain the aims of Hjalmar Schacht between 1934-7.          (30)

    b   By what means, and how successfully, did the Nazis build an economy capable of sustaining war during the period 1936-45?          (60)

## The working class

It was Hitler's aim to create a genuine **Volksgemeinschaft** (national community). However, he also wanted a disciplined work force which would not challenge his dictatorship.

- Independent unions were abolished to be replaced on 10 May 1933 by the **German Labour Front** (DAF) led by Robert Ley. In November 1933 Robert Ley established two new organisations to promote Nazi ideology amongst the working class: *Schönheit der Arbeit* (Beauty of Labour) and *Kraft durch Freude* (Strength through Joy).
- Although most workers enjoyed rising real wages after 1933 and skilled workers prospered with a return to full employment, by 1936 there was some working-class unrest, e.g. strikes at Russelheim and Berlin in 1936. However, Hitler always remained vigilant to the mood of the working classes and was aware of their apathy towards the regime, especially in Berlin.

## The middle class: the *Mittelstand*

- The *Mittelstand*, comprised of groups such as small businessmen, traders, craftsmen, clerks and shopkeepers, were Hitler's most committed supporters. From the start the regime attempted to fulfil some of its election pledges to the *Mittelstand*, e.g. the establishment of new department stores was banned on 12 May 1933 and half the consumer co-operatives were forced to close by 1935.
- After 1933, the *Mittelstand* benefited from the return of business confidence. However, their status was not significantly raised during the pre-war years. Small traders continued to be out priced by department stores and were squeezed between the Reich Food Estate, which controlled agricultural prices, and by price freezes in the shops. By 1943 a quarter of a million small shops had gone out of business.

## Rural *Volkgemeinschaft*

Nazi ideology glorified the peasant farmer and the regime attempted to safeguard small and middle-sized farmers by the **Reich Entailed Farm Law** of 29 September 1933.

- The new law identified farms of around 30 acres as being hereditary farms which had to be passed on to the eldest son without being divided up.
- Farmers were offered financial support to stay on the land and many were exempt from insurance payment.
- Farming was regulated by the **Reich Food Estate** which became a huge organisation. Its role was to supervise the country's 3 million farms, half

a million retail stores and 300,000 food-processing businesses. The Reich Food Estate fixed agricultural prices and wages, set production quotas, dictated crop rotation and allocated scarce resources.

## Women and family

Nazi ideology stressed that women should be confined to a purely domestic role in society.

- These ideas were advertised by the Nazi slogan of '**Kinder, Küche, Kirche**' (children, cooking, Church).
- The first step taken by the regime to bring women into line with Nazi ideology was the creation of the **Women's Front (Frauenfront)** by Robert Ley on 10 May 1933.
- Women in work came under attack. In 1933, nearly all the 19,000 female civil servants in regional and local government lost their jobs, as did around 15% of women teachers.
- However, the regime was careful not to upset the women's organisations which had so willingly joined the Women's Front. In 1934 the Minister of the Interior William Frick responded to widespread unease about the sacking of women teachers by reversing the policy at least temporarily.
- As the economic situation improved, so did the situation of women in most professions (apart from the law), despite the regime's official line on women in work. In 1930 5% of all doctors were women and by 1939 this figure had risen to 7%. Between 1933–39 the number of women working increased from 11.6 million to 14.6 million. This shows a contradiction between Nazi ideology and reality.

## Pro-natalism

Almost immediately after coming to office the regime embarked on a pro-natalist policy aimed at women.

- In 1933 **marriage loans** of up to 1000 Reichsmarks (around one-fifth of the average worker's annual pay) were offered to newly-weds on the condition that the wife would not work outside the home.
- For each child born to couples taking part in the marriage loan programme, the amount to be repaid was reduced by 25%. The marriage loans were a popular innovation and by 1937, 700,000 married couples had received a loan.
- **Family allowances** were set up to help those on low incomes. In 1935 low income families were given grants of up to 100 Reichsmarks per child. In 1938 child allowances were increased for those on incomes lower than 650 Reichsmarks a month.
- The status of mothers was raised by a series of propaganda campaigns. An example was the introduction of the **Mother's Cross** in 1939 for those with large families.
- However, despite these incentives, the **birth rate** did not respond

positively to Nazi policy. Nazi propaganda seems to have had some effect on women, but not as much as the regime would have hoped. The marriage rate went up from 516,800 in 1932 to 740,200 in 1934 but this was as much to do with the end of the depression as the introduction of marriage loans.

## Young people

The indoctrination of young people was an important element in the Nazi dictatorship. To establish a '1000-year Reich' Hitler aimed to educate all young people 'in the spirit of National Socialism'. The aim of such education was to train young people into certain roles: boys into soldiers; girls into submissive wives and devoted mothers. To achieve these aims the regime first encouraged from 1933, and then conscripted from 1939, German youth into huge state-run organisations.

- **Boys**. From 1933, boys aged 10–14 years old joined the **Deutsches Jungvolk** (DJ or German Young People). When aged 14 they joined the **Hitler Jugend** (HJ or Hitler Youth). From 1933 the leader of the HJ, **Baldur von Schirach**, was given the responsibility of co-ordinating all youths groups and bringing them under the control of the HJ. By 1935 some 60% of all German youth belonged to the HJ. However, even though all boys were expected to be members, it wasn't made compulsory until the **Hitler Youth Law** of 25 March 1939.
- **Girls**. At the age of 10 girls joined the **Jüngmadelbund** (JM or League of Young Girls) and at 14 they were expected to become members of the **Bund Deutscher Mädel** (BDM or League of German Girls). By 1936 the BDM had a membership of over 2 million girls. The rules on membership were similar to those of the HJ and until 1939 it was still not compulsory, although to opt out was frowned upon.

The Nazis also influenced the young via their formal education. The teaching profession was Nazified and teachers were encouraged to join the **National Socialist Teachers' Alliance** (NSLB). By 1937 some 97% or 320,000 teachers had joined. The Nazis insisted on a revised school curriculum as part of their attempt to control the minds of Germany's young people. The importance of sport was upgraded, as was history, biology and German Studies.

## Nazism and the Catholic Church

At the start of the dictatorship the Nazis followed a policy of conciliation and compromise with the Church.

- By the **Concordat** of 1933, signed between Catholic Church and state, the Catholic Church was guaranteed religious freedom and the right to conduct its own affairs without interference from the state.
- Its property rights were guaranteed, as was the legal status of the clergy and the Church's role in education was assured.

140

- In return the Church promised that it would not interfere in politics.
- It quickly became apparent that Hitler had no respect for the Concordat. However, his frustration was that the Church survived as an alternative focus for the loyalty of many Germans.
- So, in 1935 the Nazis created a **Ministry of Church Affairs** which weakened the position of the Church. However, by the end of 1935, the Catholic organisational network remained intact. Yet relations with the regime were far from secure and in a speech to the SS at Vogelsang Castle in 1937, Hitler attacked those who gave their allegiance to other organisations than the Party.

The Catholic Church's hierarchy was increasingly concerned about Hitler's attitude to organised religion. In response to growing censorship of the Catholic press and harassment of the clergy, the Papacy decided to speak out.

- On 14 March 1937, Pope Pius XI issued a Papal encyclical letter with the title **Mit Bremender Sorge** (*With Deep Anxiety*).
- Hitler's response was immediate. Religious affairs were removed from the Ministry for Church Affairs and handed to the SS. He demanded that all Germans make a choice between their religion and the regime, e.g. the ranks of the Nazi Party were closed to all but Hitler Youth graduates.
- Even though the campaign against the Church eased for the first 2 years of the war, the tension between Church and state remained. On 22 March 1941 Cardinal von Galen led an attack on the policy of executing mentally ill people. Galen's outburst resulted in an end to the euthanasia programme. However, the Catholic Church failed to speak out against the murder of Europe's Jews.

## The German Christian Church

In 1933 the Protestant faith was divided into 28 churches with 45 million members. These divisions gave Hitler the opportunity to impose his will on the Protestant Churches.

- On 4 April 1933, Hitler appointed **Ludwig Müller** as National Bishop to lead all Protestants in an all-embracing German Christian Church.
- On 14 July a new constitution for the new Church was recognised by the Reichstag. Müller was formally endorsed as the first Reich Bishop after a rigged vote. However, the ideology of this new Church was dominated as much by Nazi ideas as by Protestantism.

## Pastor Martin Niemöller and the Confessional Church

As a result of the creation of the German Christian Church, 200 pastors started a breakaway church, the Confessional Church, in 1934. In all some 7,000 of the 17,000 pastors in Germany joined the Church. Its leaders included **Pastor Martin Niemöller**, who insisted that the Church be independent of the state. He helped set up and lead the **Pastor's Emergency**

**League** in 1934 – an organisation committed to defending the new Church. In 1937, Niemöller spoke out against the regime in a sermon and was arrested and imprisoned in Dachau. During the remaining years of the Third Reich, the Confessional Church opposed the regime's attacks on religion. During the war, the Protestant Churches continued to fail to speak out against the regime. However, there were examples of individuals, such as Dietrich Bonhöffer, who showed the courage and the conviction to speak out and resist.

## Anti-Semitism

At the heart of Nazi ideology was anti-Semitism.

- After coming to power in January 1933, the Nazis moved to identify and isolate Germany's half a million Jews, discriminate against them with legislation and then attack them with propaganda and physical violence. Almost immediately after Hitler became Chancellor in January 1933, Nazis began attacks against Jews and their property.
- The regime agreed to a nation-wide **boycott** of Jewish businesses on 1 April 1933. However, the boycott was not universally popular. But throughout 1933 the Nazi leadership responded to pressure from its rank and file to act against Jews, e.g. on 7 April Jews were banned from jobs in the civil service.
- In April 1933 the Law Against the Overcrowding of Jewish Schools limited the number of Jewish students to 1.5% of the total number of young people being educated. This was in response to the exclusion of Jews from schools at a local level.

## Violence and the Nuremberg Laws, 1934–35

Propaganda against the Jews flourished after January 1933, e.g. in the pages of the widely circulated *Der Stürmer*, edited by the anti-Semite, Julius Streicher. But by 1934 Nazi leaders were again becoming disturbed by the level of locally-inspired anti-Jewish violence. Attacks against Jewish businesses damaged the regimes' standing abroad and threatened the economic recovery. But Party activists continued to demand the removal of Jews from German society. The response of Hitler was to have his civil service draft what became known as the **Nuremberg Laws** of 15 September 1935. The main points of these laws were as follows:

- The **Reich Citizenship Laws** deprived Jews of their German citizenship and their political rights.
- Under the **Law for the Protection of German Blood and German Honour** marriage and sexual relations between Jews and Germans were outlawed.

## Further discrimination, 1936–38

Following the Nuremberg Laws there was a quiet period for the Jews of

Germany. Fear of a boycott of the **1936 Berlin Olympic Games** and a wish to ensure the success of the Second Four Year Plan in its first year meant that open attacks on Jews were discouraged. However, harassment of Jews continued at a local level and decrees continued to be passed discriminating against the Jews.

- In October 1936 a decree was passed banning all civil servants from consulting Jewish doctors.
- As the economic position of Germany improved from mid-1937, so attacks on Jews worsened and intensified.
- The Anschluss in March 1938 unleashed a wave of attacks against Jewish property in Austria. This triggered Göring into issuing the **Decree for the Registration of Jewish Property** in April 1938.
- Furthermore, Jewish professionals were again attacked, e.g. from September 1938 Jewish doctors were forbidden to treat Aryan patients.

## *Kristallnacht* and its aftermath, November 1938

The murder of a German diplomat, **Ernst von Rath** in Paris, on 7 November 1938 by a Jew, **Hersch Grynszpan**, sparked an episode of violent persecution.

- The propaganda Minister Joseph Göbbels encouraged the attack on Jewish shops, homes and synagogues that became known as *Kristallnacht* (Crystal Night – because of the broken glass strewn across the pavements and streets of German towns and cities).
- Around 100 Jews were murdered and a further 20,000 were sent to concentration camps.
- After Kristallnacht the regime introduced new measures against the Jews, including the decree issued on 12 November which excluded Jews from German economic life, all Jewish pupils were expelled from school (15 November 1938) and Jewish businesses were closed (3 December 1938). Many Jews emigrated from Germany but many more stayed.
- After the Anschluss, Reinhard Heydrich set up the 'Central Office for Jewish Emigration', which was administered by **Adolf Eichmann**. In its first 6 months of operation, it forced 45,000 Jews to leave Austria.
- In January 1939, Göring set up a 'Reich Central Office for Jewish Emigration' which had been placed under the control of Reinhard Heydrich. However, events were soon to be overshadowed by the coming of war.

## The isolation of German Jews

In his infamous speech to the Reichstag on 30 January 1939, Hitler predicted that any future war would lead to 'the destruction of the Jewish race in Europe'. The concentration of Jews in specified areas began early in the war.

- In many of the conquered territories, Jews were put into recreated medieval **ghettos** (area separated off by walls).
- In January 1940 Jews were used for slave labour and confined to ghettos in the previously Polish towns of Lodz, Warsaw, Lublin, Radom and Lvov.
- By the summer of 1940, Heydrich was suggesting emigration of the 3.25 million Jews under German control to a suitable territory. The response of the Jewish section of the Foreign Office was to displace the Jews to Madagascar.
- However, the alternative of mass murder was also being considered.

## The Einsatzgruppen

The link between the war against the Soviet Union and genocide is clear.
- In March 1941 Hitler claimed that war with Russia would be one of annihilation and in the same month Heidrich wrote in a letter about the impending Final Solution, whilst also encouraging plans for Jewish emigration.
- In June, as Nazi troops swept across the western Soviet Union, SS *Einsatzgruppen* (special units set up to carry out the Final Solution) were authorised by Hitler to exterminate Jews in Russia. Eight months later 700,000 Jews had been murdered.
- In anticipation of the Holocaust, the Nazis began to convert Auschwitz into an extermination camp in the summer of 1941.

## The Wansee Conference

- On 31 July 1941, Göring ordered Heydrich to prepare for the 'sought-for final solution of the Jewish question' and in August Eichmann informed the foreign office that Jews were no longer permitted to emigrate from German-held territory.
- A conference was called to discuss the 'Jewish Question'. It met at Wansee in Berlin in January 1942. Chaired by Heydrich, it reviewed the possible alternatives for the removal of Jews from German territory including the emigration option, which was now not considered possible.
- In December 1941, the United States of America had entered the war against Germany and the war in the Soviet Union had ground to a halt. The 'solution' was to murder the Jews of Europe by working or gassing them to death. The conference ordered the organisation of the extermination of Europe's 11 million Jews.

# Assessment: German society, race and beliefs, 1933–45

## Questions in the style of Edexcel (Unit 1)

Study Sources A to D below and then answer the questions which follow.

**Source A** Adapted from a speech by Dr Auguste Reber-Gruber (consultant in the Ministry of Education) 1934 and quoted in *Mothers in the Fatherland* by Claudia Koonz, 1987.

> The female mind differs from the male mind, which excludes inwards involvement and takes a cool, businesslike pride in its 'objective' attitude. Owing to her natural disposition, her greater reverence for life, woman has the capacity for that inner devotion which more deeply fathoms the nature of things and perceives their true value and substance by means of loving absorption.

**Source B** Adapted from a speech by Vice-Chancellor von Papen made in 1933 and quoted in John Wheeler-Bennett's edited volume *Documents on International Affairs*, 1934.

> What the battlefield was for the man, motherhood was for the woman ... The maintenance of eternal life demanded the sacrifice of the individual. Mothers must exhaust themselves in order to give life to children. Fathers must fight on the battlefield in order to secure a future for their sons ... A man who is not a father is not a man ... Even more true is the saying that she who is not a mother is not a woman.

**Source C** Adapted from *Frauern: German Women recall the Third Reich*, a collection of interviews edited by Alison Owings, 1993.

> What you did NOT do, Karma said scornfully, was to emulate the Nazi vision of beauty, sex, or culture. 'Women under Hitler: that was something completely dreadful. A German woman does not wear make-up, she does not smoke, she should have a thousand children – all that rubbish, so prudish and hypocritical, it still brings a chill to my spine.'

**Source D** Adapted from *Weimar and Nazi Germany, 1919–1945*, by Martin Collier and Philip Pedley, 2000.

> Many women were easily seduced by the Nazi rhetoric that glorified their exalted status as wives and mothers. Marriages increased by 130,000 per annum and births by over half a million per annum between 1933 and 1939. Women were barred from professional employment and one-sixth had left all employment by 1937. Nazi women's organisations such as 'National Socialist Womanhood' and 'German Women's Enterprise' were enthusiastically supported.

**Q 1a** **Study Source A. From this source explain why Dr Reber-Gruber was keen to stress that 'the female mind differs from the male mind'.** **(3)**

**How to answer this question**

To gain high marks, you must try to show that you understand the quotation in the context of Nazi policy towards women. An understanding of Nazi education policy and the development of a separate curriculum for girls would be useful.

**Q b** **Use your own knowledge to explain the ways in which the Nazi regime communicated its beliefs about the role of women.** **(4)**

**How to answer this question**

To gain full marks you need to answer this question with plenty of detail from your own knowledge.

**Q c** **Study Source B. How useful is this source as evidence about attitudes towards women in 1933?** **(5)**

**How to answer this question.**

There is advice on how to answer questions about the utility of sources on page 11. In this example, note that Vice-Chancellor von Papen was a conservative, Catholic aristocrat who helped bring Hitler to power. In return he was made Hitler's Vice-Chancellor in the Cabinet created in 1933.

You need to balance the positive points and the limitations of this source in your analysis. Here is an extract from an answer to this question.

> This source is most useful in showing that Nazi attitudes towards women appealed to traditional and conservative interests. Von Papen is representative of an establishment class which believed very much that 'she who is not a mother is not a woman'.

**Q    d Study Sources C and D. Compare the impact of Nazi propaganda on women as shown by these sources and explain the differences.** (6)

### How to answer this question

There is advice on how to answer questions which ask you to compare sources on page 12. To be rewarded with a high mark you need to:
- make sure that you point out any similarities, as well as the differences between the sources
- use your own knowledge to compare
- highlight the difference in the nature of the sources and the perspective of the authors.

Here is an extract from a good answer to this question. The candidate attempted to point out and explain the differences between the sources.

> The sources differ greatly when discussing the effect Nazi propaganda had on women. In Source C the author gives the view that propaganda was ineffective. She argues that to tow the Nazi line was something 'you did NOT do'. This clearly contrasts with the assertion of Source D that women 'were easily seduced by Nazi rhetoric'. The difference stems from the perspective of the authors. The author of Source C is recounting a personal experience and writing from a personal perspective. This very much contrasts with the more generalised account of the text book.

**Q    e Use your own knowledge, and any two of the sources, to explain the Nazis' policy on women in the period 1933–39.** (12)

### How to answer this question

Advice on how to achieve a top mark on this type of question can be found on page 14. You need to make sure that you refer to all the sources and that you use your own knowledge clearly.

In the extract below, the candidate has referred to one of the sources, has evaluated the evidence and has used her own knowledge.

Nazi women's organisations such as 'National Socialist Womanhood' and 'German Women's Enterprise' were enthusiastically supported. Such support, however, represented not so much a social revolution as an attempt to return to traditional values. That traditional views were widely held can seen in the speech by von Papen (Source B) in which he encourages women to 'exhaust themselves in order to give life to children'. This source is a reliable piece of evidence, despite the suspicion that von Papen wanted to please the Nazis in 1933 and would, in public at least, echo their ideology.

## Questions in the style of Edexcel (Unit 3)

Study Source E below and then answer the questions which follow.

**Source E** Adapted from extracts from *The Wandering Jew*, a Nazi propaganda film of 1940.

The civilised Jew that we know in Germany only gives us half the picture of their racial character. This film shows genuine shots of the Polish ghettos ... We recognise that here there lies a plague spot which threatens the health of the Aryan people ... Rarely will you find a Jew engaged in useful work ... For Jews, business is a kind of holy transaction. How he earns his living is a matter of complete indifference to him ... The Jews are a race without farmers or manual workers – a race of parasites! Comparable with the wanderings of Jews through history are the mass migrations of an equally restless animal, the rat.

**Q 2a Study Source E. In what ways does the source reflect Nazi attitudes towards the Jews?** (5)

## How to answer this question

This question requires you to show the skill of comprehension. You need to make sharp and well-supported points which show that you understand clearly the viewpoint shown in the source.

Here is an extract from an answer to this question. Note how the candidate makes the point and then backs it up by quoting from the source.

The Nazis were obsessed with the identification of Jews. Their fear as reflected in this source was the assimilated Jew who was not so easily identifiable, or as the source describes 'gives us half the picture'.

**Q b Explain how the Nazis persecuted the Jews between 1933–39.** (7)

## How to answer this question

This question asks for a detailed explanation. To gain top marks you must show that you understand how the regime persecuted Jews in different ways and in phases.

You must plan your answer clearly before you start. Here are examples of the type of point you might make in your plan:
- how the Nazis persecuted the Jews depended on political circumstances.
- Jews were persecuted through legislation, discrimination and violence.

Here is an extract from an answer written in an appropriate style.

> The nature of the persecution of the Jews changed with circumstances. Before the 1936 Berlin Olympics persecution was kept to a minimum because of the fear of a boycott of the Games. As the economic position of Germany improved from mid-1937, so economic persecution of the Jews intensified. Those who feared the economic results of attacks on the Jews looked to the Minister of Economics, Hjalmar Schacht to argue their case. In November 1937 he was forced to resign his post. In December 1937 Hermann Göring ordered that Jewish businesses be restricted in the raw materials they could receive. The Anschluss in March 1938 triggered Göring into issuing the Decree for the Registration of Jewish Property in April 1938. Furthermore, the Jewish professionals were again attacked, e.g. from September 1938 Jewish doctors were forbidden to treat Aryan patients. Such economic persecution took place only after an improvement in economic circumstances.

**Q    c   What are the reasons for the persecution of the Jews in Germany in the years 1933–39?**                                    **(18)**

## How to answer this question

To gain top marks on this question you need to sustain an analytical line throughout the answer. You must be very clear about the line of argument you are going to take. Here are some examples of key points that you could put into your plan and then develop throughout your answer:
- the Jews were persecuted primarily because anti-Semitism was at the heart of Nazi philosophy
- the Nazi regime used persecution as the means by which it could control the Party
- persecution also was the product of power politics within the regime.

Here is an example of a direct answer to this style of question.

Often persecution was undertaken for political purposes. A very obvious example of this was the Nuremberg Laws which were devised in 1935 to rally Party morale and to please the SA – a restless faction within the movement. Nazi radicals were disappointed by the moderation of the regime and were uneasy about the alliance with conservatives such as Schacht. Often they would use persecution for opportunist reasons. Joseph Göbbels' staunch anti-Semitism led him to have access to Hitler. In November 1938, after losing favour following his affair with Lida Baarova, he sought to recover his position by directing the Krystallnacht attack.

## Further question in the style of Edexcel (Unit 3)

Study Source A and then answer the following question.

**Source A** Adapted from the speech given by Adolf Hitler to the Reichstag on 30 January 1939.

Europe cannot find peace until the Jewish question has been solved. It may well be that sooner or later an agreement may be reached in Europe itself between nations who otherwise would not find it so easy to arrive at an understanding. There still exists sufficient land available on this globe. Today I will once more be a prophet: if the international Jewish financiers in and outside Europe should succeed in plunging the nations once more into a world war, then the result will [be] ....the annihilation of the Jewish race in Europe.

Q  3a  **Study Source A. What, according to Source A, is Hitler's attitude towards the Jews by January 1939?**                    (5)
   b  **What, in the years 1933–39 were the main aims of Nazi policy against Germany's Jewish population?**                    (7)
   c  **What impact did Nazi racial policy have on German society between 1935 and 1939?**                    (18)

# Section 7: The Nazi State and consolidation of power

### The Reichstag fire and its aftermath

Those who believed that they had 'tamed' Hitler and his movement were to be proved very much mistaken. Although his 'Appeal to the German People' broadcast on 1 February was conservative in nature, the SA began to take revenge on the enemies of National Socialism. On 27 February, the Reichstag building in Berlin was gutted by fire. The Nazis exploited real fears of a Communist-led uprising to justify a clamp down on the left (including the arrest of KPD politicians). They also persuaded President Hindenberg to issue the decree '**For the Protection of People and State**' which ended the civil liberties guaranteed in the Weimar constitution.

### Election March 1933

Despite a campaign of irregularity and intimidation organised by Joseph Göbbels, the Nazis failed to win an absolute majority, polling 43.9%. However, the Nazis achieved a majority by the support of the nationalist DNVP, whose 52 seats were added to the 288 won by the Nazis. Communist KPD deputies were barred from the Reichstag (despite their 4.8 million votes), the result giving Hitler a distinct political advantage.

### Hitler seeks legality

However, Hitler was not yet the dictator he wanted to be. To change the constitution he needed the support of two-thirds of the Reichstag, which he did not have. He was keen to impress Hindenberg and the wider establishment that he could control the more **radical elements** in the Nazi movement. On 21 March 1933, Hitler held an impressive display of his legality and respectability at the ceremonial opening of the Reichstag which was held in Potsdam. However, Hitler's real intentions were more clearly seen in a piece of legislation was introduced the same day. The **Malicious Practices Law** banned criticism of the regime and its policies.

### The Enabling Act, 1933

The opening for business of the new Reichstag on 23 March 1933 was marked by the presentation of an **Enabling Act**. By the terms of the Act, the government gave the power to pass laws to the Cabinet and allowed the government to alter the constitution as it saw fit. It granted Hitler 4 years of power as a dictator. It was overwhelmingly passed by 441 to 94. This was achieved because the communist deputies were banned and the Nazis won the support of the Centre Party. The Weimar constitution was dead.

### *Gleichschaltung* (co-ordination)

As part of the consolidation of Nazi power, Hitler attempted to co-ordinate all aspects of German political and social life under Nazi control.

- **Local government** On 31 March all state parliaments (diets) were dissolved by the Minister of the Interior, Wilhelm Frick, with the exception of the diet of Prussia. New state governors, **Reichsstadthalter**, were appointed with full powers to introduce Nazi policies. The centralisation of the state was completed in January 1934 with the abolition of the upper house of the Reichstag (the Reichsrat), and the provincial governments and the local governments were made completely subordinate to the central government.
- **Civil service** By the Law for the Restoration of the Professional Civil Service of 7 April 1933, Jews and political opponents of the Nazis were thrown out of the civil service. To bring the running of Party and state closer together, the Nazis passed the Law to Ensure the Unity of Party and State on 1 December 1933.
- **The German Labour Front** On 2 May 1933 the offices of all unions were taken over and trade unions were banned. On 10 May the **German Labour Front** (DAF) was established under Robert Ley's leadership.
- **Abolition of political parties** The process of creating a dictatorship also included the disbanding of all other political parties. After the Reichstag fire the communist KPD had been outlawed. In June 1933 the SPD was banned and the DNP, DVP and DNVP disbanded. To avoid confrontation with the Nazis, the Centre Party followed suit on 5 July. The actions of the parties made it easier for Hitler to abolish organised political opposition with the 'Law against the Formation of Parties' of 14 July 1933.

## The run up to the 'Night of the Long Knives'

- By the spring of 1934 Hitler's dictatorship seemed secure. However, conservative forces threatened Hitler in business, the civil service and, above all, in the army. Many conservatives were alarmed at the lawlessness of the Nazi government actions of the SA particularly.
- Hitler felt threatened by the personal ambitions of **Ernst Röhm** who was leader of the 2 million-strong SA. Röhm's plans to amalgamate the SA and *Reichswehr* to form a People's Army under his leadership also alarmed the military establishment.
- In April 1934, a group of leading generals, led by General Walther von Brauchitsch, issued an ultimatum that the Army would only support the Nazi regime if the SA were purged.
- At Marberg in June 1934 Vice-Chancellor von Papen called for an end to SA violence. Hitler was acutely aware that these conservative groups were still politically important because they had President Hindenberg's ear. Hitler was encouraged by Göring and Himmler to take decisive action against Röhm.

## The 'Night of the Long Knives'

With the excuse that the SA was on the verge of uprisings in Berlin and Munich, Hitler ordered a purge of the leadership of the SA to take place on 30 June 1934. Around 400 potential political opponents were killed including Röhm, ex-Chancellor von Schleicher and an old rival of Hitler's, Gregor Strasser. The 'Night of the Long Knives' was a vital step for the Nazis on the road to the consolidation of power. Despite the murder of General von Schleicher, the 'Night of the Long Knives' resulted in a closer alliance between Nazi State and Army.

## Hitler becomes Führer

Upon the peaceful death of President Hindenberg on August 2, Hitler was able to abolish the position of Presidency, assuming all powers for himself as Führer (leader) of the German State. On the initiative of the Minister of Defence, Field Marshal **Werner von Blomberg**, all officers of the army were called on to take a personal oath of loyalty to the Führer. This was of critical importance in securing the dictatorship. On 19 August a plebiscite (vote) was held. The German people were asked to show whether they approved of Hitler becoming Führer. The result was a great victory for Nazi propaganda, 43.06 million Germans voted and of this figure 89.93% voted 'yes' in favour of Hitler.

## The army

- The army was the most powerful non-Nazi force in the dictatorship. Whilst some generals looked down on Hitler because of his background and his rank, many were sympathetic towards his nationalist views, anti-communist stance and plans for rearmament.
- The appointment of General von Blomberg as Minister of Defence in January 1933 secured Hitler's alliance with the army.
- After the 'Night of the Long Knives' the army was in a stronger position. The army's confidence in the regime increased with the development of the rearmament programme and the introduction of conscription in March 1935. However, despite the re-militarisation of the Rhineland in 1936 there were still tensions between army and regime.

## Hossbach and the Blomberg-Fritsch affair

- At the **Hossbach Conference** in 1937 (the record of which is known as the **Hossbach Memorandum**) Hitler put forward his foreign policy aims. High on the list was the recovery of German lands and peoples lost at Versailles, and lebensraum (living space) in the east.
- Some generals including von Blomberg, Ludwig Beck and Werner von Fritsch raised doubts about Germany's ability to fight any war. Hitler acted angrily to what he saw as criticism and he moved against those he perceived as his enemies.

- In February 1938, the Minister of Defence and supreme commander of the Wehrmacht, Field Marshall von Blomberg was forced to resign when Berlin police files revealed that his wife might have worked as a prostitute in the past. On Blomberg's dismissal, Hitler appointed himself Supreme Commander of the armed forces.
- Another opponent of Hitler's at Hossbach, General von Fritsch, was forced to resign at the same time over accusations that he had been involved in homosexual acts. Hitler appointed the ever-loyal General Keitel as Chief of the High Command and Field Marshall Walther von Brauchitsch as Commander in Chief of the army. Both had limited powers. To complete the purge, 16 generals were retired and 44 transferred.

## Resistance

- Despite the purge, General Beck did attempt to lead a putsch against Hitler during the Czech Crisis of September 1938 which he believed might trigger a war against Britain and France. It was foiled when Britain and France gave in to Hitler's claims at Munich.
- After 1940, more generals joined the resistance including Hans Oster (Chief of Staff, military intelligence), Franz Halder (Chief of the Army's General Staff, 1938–42), Karl von Stülpnagel (Military Governor of France), Erich Fellgiebel (Chief of Communications for the Armed Forces) and leading officers Henning von Trescow and Claus von Stauffenberg.
- In March 1943, two officers attempted to assassinate Hitler by placing a time bomb on his plane. Known as Operation Flash, the attempt on Hitler's life was masterminded by Major General von Tresckow. The attempt failed when the detonator did not go off.

## The Kreisau Circle and the July Plot, 1944

As the war turned against Germany, so more members of the military establishment were drawn together in opposition to the Nazi leadership:
- The most significant group was the '**Kreisau Circle**' led by Helmuth von Moltke and Peter von Watenburg. In August 1943, they drew up their **Basic principles for the New Order** which was a blueprint for a new German State based on democratic values.
- By 1943 the group had some 20 members including social democrat Julius Leber and Deitrich Bonhöffer. From the ranks of the Kreisau Circle came many of the conspirators in '**Operation Valkyrie**', the most serious attempt to assassinate Hitler. The aim of the plot was to replace Hitler with a provisional government led by General Beck.
- On 20 July 1944 a bomb left by Claus von Stauffenberg exploded at Hitler's headquarters at Rastenberg. Unfortunately for the conspirators, the briefcase carrying the bomb had been moved from its position where it might well have killed Hitler. As a result Hitler suffered only

minor injuries. Some 200 conspirators were ruthlessly tracked down, arrested and executed. The list of those killed included von Staffenberg, Beck, Dr Leber, Father Alfred Delp and Admiral Wilhelm Canaris.

## The central role of Hitler in the Nazi state

In the Nazi State, Hitler made laws. He was the supreme master of the Nazi state. Around him were many institutions, which competed for his attention and influence. As the state developed, so laws were increasingly made by **Führer decrees (Erlasse)** which Hitler would sign, or by **Führer orders** that were spoken. Hitler's authority came from his position at the centre of the Nazi movement. His was the final word in any dispute and in all policies he considered essential, Hitler made the key decisions – from the 'Night of the Long Knives' in 1934 to the invasion of Poland in 1939 and the launching of the Final Solution in 1941. The problem was that at a lower decision-making level, Hitler's orders were often contradictory. It is clear that the Nazi state was not a well-ordered monolithic structure but a collection of competing bureaucracies and power blocs over which Hitler presided. He remained the source of ideology and the arbiter of all decisions. In this sense he was a strong dictator.

## The decline of Cabinet government

The traditional means of running the country was by Cabinet government. In the first year, Hitler accepted the Cabinet as the formal means of government and in 1933 it met 72 times. However, by 1936 the Cabinet only met four times. Slowly, Hitler removed from influence all those who were not Nazis. In 1937 and 1938, the last of the conservatives were removed, e.g. Hjalmar Schacht was sacked as Minister of Economics in November 1937. The decline in the Cabinet meant that there was a vacuum at the heart of the Nazi State. This vacuum was filled by the Reich Chancellery which drew up legislation. The Head of the Chancellery, **Hans-Heinrich Lammers**, took this Cabinet role as the co-ordinator of government. The Chancellery's position at the heart of government was weakened by new ministries, which tended to act more independently than the old traditional ministries, e.g. the SS or the Four Year Plan office.

## Hess and Bormann

From 1934 Hitler gave the '**Führer's Deputy for Party Affairs**', **Rudolf Hess**, and, indirectly, his Chief of Staff **Martin Bormann** more personal power. Hess, for example, had the power to supervise new laws.

- As a result, Hess and Bormann succeeded in asserting the dominance of the Party over the state civil service. Bormann set up his own Party organisation which rivalled that of the Reich Chancellery. Hess managed to strengthen the Party's position before 1939.
- The war saw this trend continue with the Party reaching new heights of power and influence.

- In September 1939 leading Gauleiters became Reich Defence Commissioners and began to assume total control in their regions.
- In May 1941, Hess flew to Scotland in an attempt to make peace with Britain. This left Bormann with considerably greater influence in charge of the Party Chancellery. He formed the Committee of Three with Keitel and Lammers and attempted to use this to try to isolate rivals.

## Bormann's power

In 1943, Bormann became Hitler's personal secretary – the **Führer's Secretary** – which again strengthened the Party in its relations with the State. However, much of Bormann's energies were spent trying to protect his position and influence from the challenges of Albert Speer and Heinrich Himmler. As a close friend of Hitler and the mastermind behind the mobilisation of the economy, Speer shared Bormann's access to Hitler. In 1943, Bormann tried to turn the Gauleiters against Speer but the attempt failed to undermine Hitler's confidence in his favourite minister. Such rivalry weakened the Nazi state.

## The influence of the SS

The SS was the most powerful and most sinister element of the Nazi movement. Originally formed as Hitler's elite bodyguard in 1925, it was turned into a formidable private army by its leader **Heinrich Himmler**. The SS were the racial elite of the Nazi Party. After the 'Night of the Long Knives' in June 1934, the SS took control of the concentration camp system and became the main police arm of the Nazi Party with the aim of eliminating all opposition within the state. This task became the specific responsibility of the **SS Security Service (SD)** and the **Gestapo**.
- **The SD** was formed by Himmler in March 1934 and was placed under the command of Reinhard Heydrich. It was the intelligence arm of the SS with the special task of maintaining the security of Führer, Party leadership, Nazi Party and Reich. Throughout the Nazi regime it had the power of arrest, detention and execution.
- The **Gestapo** undertook the role of a secret police force. In April 1933, Göring incorporated the Prussian political police into the Gestapo and set them up in their new offices on the Prince Albertstrasse in Berlin. In April 1934, Göring appointed Himmler Head of the unified political police force. This was important as it gave Himmler and the SS some control over the state police. In 1936 any confusion was resolved – Hitler appointed Himmler Head of the German Police. In 1939 the Reich Security Head Office (RSHA) was formed, which brought together the Gestapo and SD under the central leadership of the SS. By 1939, in its role as the political police force the Gestapo became the most important element in the State's security system. It played a key role in eliminating opposition through creating an elaborate terror machine.

How to Pass AS Modern World History

# Assessment: The Nazi State and consolidation of power

## Questions in the style of AQA (Unit 3)

Q  **How important were the events of 1934 in ensuring the Nazi consolidation of power?**

### How to answer this question

This question asks you to analyse the events of 1934. The emphasis of the essay must be on 1934 and you are advised to focus on this year first. You should plan your essay to avoid simply running through a narrative account of 1934. Most importantly you must try to identify points of argument. Here is an example:
- the events of 1934 were crucial to the consolidation of power
- the elites were increasingly marginalised
- the de-stabilising effect of the SA removed
- the support of the army for the Fuhrer was assured.

In answering the question you should make reference to the following topics:
- the Night of the Long Knives
- the death of Hindenburg
- the army's oath of loyalty
- the 1934 plebiscite.

## Question in the style of OCR (Unit 1)

Read the source and answer the questions that follow.

**Source A** Adapted from Hitler's speech to Reich Governors, July 1933.

The political parties have now been abolished. The achievement of outward power must be followed by the inward education of man.

Revolution is not a permanent state, it must not develop into a lasting state. The full spate of revolution must now be guided into the secure bed of evolution. We must not keep looking round to see what next to revolutionise. The main thing now is not programmes or ideas but the daily bread of five million people.

**Source B** From Hitler's *Appeal to the German People*, January 1933.

The National Government will, therefore, regard it as its first and supreme task to restore to the German people unity of mind and will. It will take under its firm protection Christianity as the basis of our morality, and the family as the nucleus of our nation and our State. It will bring back to our people the consciousness of its racial and political unity. It wishes to base the education of German youth on respect for our great past. Germany must not and will not sink into communist anarchy. In place of our turbulent instincts it will make national discipline govern our life.

The National Government will carry out the great task of reorganising our national economy with two big Four Year Plans:
- saving the German farmer so that the nation's food supply and thus the life of the nation shall be secured
- saving the German worker by a massive attack on unemployment.

**Source C** From Hitler's speech to the Reichstag in March 1936 after the re-militarisation of the Rhineland.

You know how hard was the road that I have had to travel since January 1933 in order to free the German people from the dishonourable position in which it found itself. At no moment of my struggle on behalf of the German people have I forgotten the duty incumbent on me to uphold European cultures and European civilisation. The German people have no interest in seeing the French people suffer. Why should it not be possible to lift the problem of conflicting interests between European States above the sphere of passion and unreason and consider it in the calm light of a higher vision?

**Source D** Taken from a memorandum written by Hitler in August 1936.

The world has been moving with ever-increasing speed towards a new conflict, the cause of which is Bolshevism.
I thus set the following tasks:
1  The German armed forces must be operational within four years.
2  The German economy must be fit for war within four years.

**Q 1a** Study Source A. Using the source and your own knowledge, explain why Hitler stressed in January 1933 that 'revolution is not a permanent state; it must not develop into a lasting state'. **(12)**

## How to answer this question

To gain a top mark you need to show that you understand the source in its historical context. In particular you must show that you have a clear understanding of Hitler's need to reassure the conservative élites including the army. The remark in the quote is also directly aimed at Röhm and the more radical elements of the SA.

**Q b** Study Source B. How useful is this source to an historian studying Hitler's intentions as Germany's leader in 1933? **(24)**

## How to answer this question

This question requires you to make an evaluation about the utility of the source. It would be helpful to refer to the checklist on pages 10–11.

Before you start writing this answer you should make a brief plan. Here are the type of points you might include in a plan.
- **Positive points** The source reflects Hitler's political priorities, the points that he felt appealed to German people in 1933.
- **Limitations** The speech is a formal one to a national audience very soon after Hitler had come to power. Therefore it is not particularly revealing of many intentions.
- **Reliability** Purpose of the source was to gain votes in the March 1933 elections and to persuade German populace of the conservatism of the new regime, therefore the message was distorted.

Here is an example of the style you might use when answering this question. Note that the student who wrote this response is answering the question directly and has used his/her own information to back up the point made.

> However, the source has many limitations, not least the fact that the speech was part of the March 1933 election campaign. *The Appeal to the German People* was made to calm conservative fears of the revolutionary nature of the new regime. Therefore, Hitler deliberately stresses his commitment to conservative interests, e.g. the 'firm protection [of] Christianity'. Subsequent attacks on the Church after 1933 show that this was not his true intention.

**Q**   **c**  **Study Sources C and D. Compare Hitler's intentions in Sources C and D. Explain the differences between the sources.** **(36)**

## How to answer this question

To answer this question fully you must address both the similarities and the differences between the sources. Refer to the checklist on page 12 before you start writing. You need to use your own knowledge to answer the question.

You should plan briefly your answer. To gain top marks you should come to a judgement and this will form the basis of your whole answer. Here is an example of the type of planning which is necessary:
- there are fundamental differences between the sources because of their intended audiences.
- although the sources name different potential enemies, they both hold the threat of conflict.

In your answer you must ensure that you refer to the sources rather than write in general terms. As has been advised elsewhere, your quotes from the sources should be short and to the point. Here is an example of the style you might write in.

A similarity between the sources is Hitler's intended enemy. In the more reliable Source D Hitler clearly states that at the root of conflict 'is Bolshevism'. This does not contradict Hitler's suggestion in Source D that Germany had no 'interest in seeing the French people suffer'. One of Hitler's primary foreign policy objectives was indeed the destruction of the Soviet Union. However, the difference between the sources is a false one. Hitler also wished for revenge against the French for Versailles. Source C should be seen as unreliable in that the speech was public and made to reassure Britain and France in the wake of re-militarisation of the Rhineland.

**Q**   **d**  **Use all the sources and your own knowledge to answer the following question. Explain Hitler's priorities and aims as Germany's leader in the period 1933–39.** **(48)**

## How to answer this question

There are two key elements to answering a question of this type.
1  Most importantly you need to use your own knowledge to frame an answer to this question.
2  You also need to ensure that you use and evaluate all the sources, both as a collection and individually.

Because this is such an open question, your answer will have to be well planned. You need to place the sources in the context of your own knowledge. The first part of your plan should be the key points which form the basis of your argument. Here are two points that you might make:

- Hitler's aims and priorities changed with circumstances. Initially his priority was the consolidation of power. Once achieved, he turned his attentions more to the priorities of preparation for war, the destruction of Versailles and a social transformation.
- Hitler was, however, constant in his ideological objectives throughout the period in question.

Try to ensure that your answer contains the three strands of your own knowledge, source interpretation and source evaluation. Here is an extract from an answer which does all three.

> Hitler's priority was to consolidate the power of the Nazi regime. Until at least 1936 the conservative elites were placated and economic policy was geared to that purpose, e.g. the removal of the threat of the SA in 1934 and the reduction in unemployment. This is very much reflected in the sources. Source B denies that the regime is revolutionary – 'revolution is not a permanent state' – and the main issue is 'the daily bread of 5 million people'. However this source is written at a time when the regime was still not secure and can't be considered as reliable evidence of Hitler's aims or priorities across the whole period in question. However, it is most useful in showing the tactics used by the regime in the months after it had come to power.

**Further questions**

**Course essay questions in the style of AQA (Unit 3)**

Q 2 **How important were the roles played by von Papen and General von Schleicher in Hitler's appointment as Chancellor in 1933?**

Q 3 **How did the Nazis consolidate power, 1933–4?**

# Chapter 6
# The Cold War

## Section 1: International relations, 1945–89

### American policy 1944–5

American mistrust of Soviet intentions increased as the Soviet army occupied eastern Europe. The failure of the Red Army to help the Polish insurgents in the Warsaw Uprising in 1944 caused considerable concern in Washington. The agreement at the **Yalta Conference** in February 1945 was hailed as a success in the United States. President Roosevelt felt that he had secured Soviet guarantees of free elections in Poland and there was agreement on other issues including the setting up of the United Nations, the first meeting of which was to be in April 1945 in San Francisco. However on 12 April 1945 Roosevelt died. His successor **Harry S. Truman** had a markedly different attitude towards the Soviet Union as was shown in heated exchanges between Truman and Soviet Foreign Minister Molotov at the **Potsdam Conference**. In August 1945 Truman ordered the use of atomic weapons on the Japanese cities of Nagasaki and Hiroshima.

### The Iron Curtain and Kennan Report

The new hostility in the west towards the Soviet Union was reflected in Winston Churchill's speech at **Fulton, Missouri** in March 1946 in which he described Soviet domination of eastern Europe as the descent of '**an iron curtain**'. There was considerable debate in the USA in 1946 about policy towards the Soviets.
- In February 1946 a young diplomat in Moscow, **George Kennan**, sent a detailed report to Washington arguing that the Soviets posed a political and economic threat to American interests. Kennan argued that the United States should adopt a policy of 'containment' towards the Soviet Union and communism.
- Not all agreed with the proposed new tough line against the Soviet Union. In September 1946 Secretary of Commerce **Harry Wallace** was asked to resign his post for criticising the new foreign policy stance. Truman believed that isolationism was not a feasible policy.

### Truman Doctrine and Marshall Plan

In 1946, civil war in Turkey and Greece saw communists fighting to topple non-communist regimes. Truman's response was to issue the **Truman Doctrine** in March 1947. At its heart was a commitment to **contain** communism anywhere in the world. As part of this policy, Secretary of State **George Marshall** announced a huge aid programme to non-communist states in Europe. By 1952 over $13,000 million in aid had been given. By these policies and others including the creation of the Deutschemark in Germany in 1948, the divisions between Soviet-dominated and non-communist Europe became clearer. Truman's commitment to containment was highlighted by the determination of the western powers to support Berlin during the airlift in 1949.

### NATO and Korea

In April 1949 the **North Atlantic Treaty Organisation** (NATO) was formed. Dominated by the Americans, the alliance was committed to preventing the spread of communism using military force if necessary. In October 1949 Truman signed the **Mutual Assistance Act** which provided for $1 billion for the United States' new allies. The fear of communist expansion increased with the successful testing of a Soviet bomb in 1949 and a successful communist revolution in China led by Mao Tse Tung.

- In June 1950 South Korea was invaded by troops from the communist North who were attempting to reunite the country by force. The Americans intervened with the support of the United Nations and General Douglas MacArthur was appointed Commanding General.
- From July to October 1950 United Nations forces pushed the North Koreans back across the 38th parallel to the Yalu river. This action provoked the intervention of the Chinese who drove the Americans back into South Korea.
- For the next two years a war of attrition was fought until 1953 when a new American President, Ike Eisenhower, gave the political impetus necessary for a peace. Korea was divided along the 38th parallel.

### The arms race

Just as the Americans were determined to contain communism, so the Soviets were determined to protect it. The 1950s saw this conflict played out against the backdrop of a nuclear arms race.

- In 1952 the Americans exploded their first thermonuclear bomb to be followed the next year by the Soviets.
- Although there were attempts to control the proliferation of arms, for example by a voluntary suspension of the testing of nuclear weapons by both sides in 1958, the arms race continued apace. It was partly fuelled by the emerging **space** race.
- In 1957 the Soviets launched the satellite **Sputnik** which successfully orbited the earth. The Soviet success had a profound impact on American planners who feared Soviet technological superiority.

### The limits to 'peaceful coexistence'

In 1953 Stalin died. The new Soviet leader Nikita Khrushchev promised an era of 'peaceful coexistence' with the capitalist world. There were signs that a warming of relations was possible.

- In 1955 the Soviets withdrew from Austria as agreed ten years before and in the same year Khrushchev attended a successful 'great power' summit conference at Geneva. However the concept of 'peaceful coexistence' was fragile when placed against the reality of the Cold War.
- Khrushchev was committed, as was his successor, to the protection of a Soviet-dominated eastern Europe. In 1953 workers' riots in eastern Germany were crushed by Soviet tanks.
- Soviet concern about the actions of NATO led to the creation of the Warsaw Pact in 1955.
- In Poland in 1956 demonstrations led to the appointment of reformist politician Oscar Gomulka as leader of the Polish Communist Party.
- There were similar demonstrations in Hungary and widespread demands for the relaxation of the Stalinist system. In October 1956 the reformer Imre Nagy was installed as Prime Minister. However his proposals for democratic reforms resulted in a Soviet invasion in November 1956. This invasion showed the limitations of the policy of containment.

## Berlin

The deployment of short range tactical nuclear weapons in Europe heightened tension further in Germany, as did the refusal of the West to recognise East Germany. In November 1958 the Soviets proposed that West Berlin become a free demilitarised zone. They also proposed that the USSR would sign a treaty with the DDR thereby threatening Berlin's status. The east German government was concerned by the numbers of east Germans fleeing to the west via Berlin. At **Vienna** in 1961 Khruschev suggested to the new American President J F Kennedy that West Berlin should become a free city by the end of the year and access from the west would be denied. The number of refugees increased. On 13 August 1961 the East German leader **Walter Ulbrecht** ordered the building of the Berlin Wall.

## The Cuban Missile Crisis, 1962

Events in Cuba in 1962 threatened to provoke a nuclear war.
- In 1959 a communist revolution led by **Fidel Castro** toppled the American-backed government of Batista. The fact that Cuba is only 90 miles from Florida meant that the revolution caused real concern in Washington.
- Tension between the superpowers increased when the Soviets shot down an American U2 spy plane over the Soviet Union in 1960 and captured its pilot Gary Powers.
- In April 1961 an American CIA-backed invasion of Cuba failed. Known as the **Bay of Pigs** débacle it strengthened American resolve in its dealings over Cuba.
- In 1962 the Americans deployed nuclear missiles in Turkey. The Soviet response was to place missile bases in Cuba.
- The Americans demanded the removal of the missile bases and prepared

How to Pass AS Modern World History

to blockade the island. Frenzied diplomacy followed with the result that the Soviets agreed to remove their launch pads.

However the levels of tension experienced during the crisis pushed the world to the edge of nuclear warfare. In its wake a telephone '**hotline**' was set up between Washington and Moscow.

## Vietnam

The withdrawal of France from Vietnam saw the country partitioned into a communist-dominated North and a capitalist South. The invasion of the South by communist insurgents known as the **Vietcong** concerned American foreign policy observers. The dominant idea at the time was the '**domino theory**'; if one state was allowed to fall to communism then all those around would also fall.

- In 1961 President Kennedy ordered military support for the South Vietnamese government led by Ngo Dinh Diem. In 1964 this aid escalated after the Gulf of Tonkin incident in which an American destroyer was allegedly attacked by the North Vietnamese navy.
- Massive air raids and the deployment of over half a million troops in Vietnam failed to produce a victory. The communist Tet offensive in 1968 triggered considerable opposition to the war in the United States.
- The new President Nixon ordered the scaling down of land forces in Vietnam but a bombing campaign continued against communist targets in Vietnam, Cambodia and Laos.
- In January 1973 a ceasefire was called and American troops withdrew. In 1975 the South Vietnamese capital Saigon fell to the North.

## Czechoslovakia

Khrushchev was replaced as Soviet leader in 1964 by a collective leadership. In 1968 events in Czechoslovakia propelled **Leonid Brezhnev** to the forefront of the Soviet government. Student protests in Prague in 1966 had led to the appointment of a new communist leader **Alexander Dubček** in January 1968.

- Dubček proceeded to introduce a series of reforms nicknamed the '**Prague Spring**'. Such 'socialism with a human face' did not mean a rejection of the Warsaw Pact.
- However Brezhnev ordered Warsaw Pact troops into Czechoslovakia to crush the reformist movement.
- Dubček was replaced by the hard-line Husak and the Brezhnev Doctrine was born. This stated that all Warsaw Pact countries had a responsibility to intervene when communism was under threat in a member country. However there was opposition to the use of tanks in Czechoslovakia from within the communist world. Romania and Yugoslavia condemned the action and refused to take part.

## Détente

 The American failure in Vietnam signalled a shift in Cold War politics. The policy of containment had failed in South East Asia as it was to fail in post-colonial Africa. In Cambodia the **Khmer Rouge** took control under Pol Pot. Nixon and his Secretary of State **Henry Kissinger** embarked on a policy of détente.

* The **Strategic Arms Limitation Talks** 1972 (SALT 1) resulted in the signing of an agreement limiting the number of Intercontinental Ballistic Missiles.
* Better relations between the superpowers led to better relations between the two Germanys. In 1972 the **Basic Treaty** saw West Germany recognise East Germany and two years later the United States followed suit. In Helsinki in 1975 a series of accords were signed culminating in the **Final Act** which recognised Europe's borders and made certain commitments to human rights.
* However the refusal of the communist world to implement these proposals led to a cooling of relations. In the Soviet block, dissident groups such as **Charter 77** in Czechoslovakia continued to protest at the absence of human rights in their countries.

## The Second Cold War and the collapse of communism

In 1979 the Soviet Union invaded **Afghanistan** in an attempt to extend its sphere of influence. They became involved in a bloody war which lasted for ten years with little gain. The result of the conflict was an end to détente. The American Congress refused to ratify the SALT II treaty and in 1980 the United States of America boycotted the **Moscow Olympics**. Just as a change of President in the US in 1945 changed relations between East and West so the election of Ronald Reagan in 1980 was to herald a significant change in American foreign policy. Reagan initiated a new arms race with the **Strategic Defence Initiative** (Star Wars) and adopted an aggressive stance against the Soviets. Meanwhile the support for communism in the Eastern Block was being challenged.

## Poland

In 1978, Polish Cardinal Karol Wojtyla became Pope John Paul II. This was an important turning point as Wojtyla was a fierce critic of the communist regime in his homeland.

* In 1980 an independent trade union **Solidarity** led by Lech Walesa challenged the communist government to permit greater religious and political freedom.
* A new Polish government led by **General Jaruzelski** was charged with crushing the movement. In 1981 martial law was declared and leaders of the Solidarity movement were arrested.
* However repression failed to crush the movement. With international

support Solidarity continued to campaign for political freedom until 1989 when elections were organised in which they triumphed.

## The collapse of communism

The fact that Solidarity members were allowed to participate in elections in 1989 was due to the change in attitude of the Soviet leadership.

- The Soviets were forced to review policy because of the cost of the Afghanistan war, the inability of the Soviet Union to match American defence spending, and economic stagnation and decline.
- In 1985 Yuri Andropov was succeeded as General Secretary by **Michail Gorbachev**. A communist, Gorbachev believed that reform was essential if the communist system was to survive.
- He introduced policies of **perestroika** (restructuring) and **glasnost** (openness) as a means of producing change. In 1988 Gorbachev ended Soviet involvement in Afghanistan and abandoned the Brezhnev Doctrine. He also built better relations with the West. However, as the threat of Soviet intervention diminished many countries within the Soviet sphere pressed for greater political independence.
- In May 1989 the Hungarian government opened its borders to the west, an action which breached the Iron Curtain. In October 1989 the Berlin Wall was dismantled as Gorbachev promised that the Soviet army would not intervene to prevent reform. In the next two months, communist governments fell in Czechoslovakia, Romania and East Germany.

# Assessment: International relations, 1945–89

## Questions in the style of AQA (Unit 1)

Read Source A and answer the questions which follow.

**Source A** Adapted from a speech made by President Truman on 12 March 1947. The ideas in this speech later became known as the Truman Doctrine.

> I believe that it must be the policy of the United States to support free people who are resisting conquest by armed minorities or outside pressures.

**Q 1a Explain what Truman means by 'free people' in the context of the years which followed the Second World War.** **(3)**

### How to answer this question

The question asks you to explain fully what Truman meant by freedom. In particular you should mention democracy, self determination and the threats to them both in post-war Europe.

**Q b Explain why Truman made this speech at this time.** **(7)**

### How to answer this question

To receive a top level mark for answering this question you must try to do the following:
- prioritise the reasons why Truman made this speech
- link the long and short term causes of the Truman Doctrine.

It would be worth listing your main points of explanation. Below are examples of the key points which could be made in response to the question.
- Truman's speech summed up the change in American foreign policy brought about by events in Europe in 1946.
- The Truman Doctrine emerged from the collapse of the wartime alliance, a change in presidency and the tension of Potsdam.

Here is an example of an extract from an answer to this question. You should note the attempt of the candidate to prioritise factors.

> Without doubt the most important reason for the speech which became known as the Truman Doctrine was the emergence of a hard line anti-Soviet attitude in Washington. This attitude, as reflected by George Kennan's 'long telegram' matched Truman's anti-communist instincts. His hatred of communism and mistrust of Stalin's intentions in Europe and beyond was seen most clearly at Potsdam.

**Q** c **How successful was the United States' policy of supporting 'free people who are resisting conquest' in the period 1945–53?** (15)

### How to answer this question

You need to focus on the question of success. There must be some form of judgement made in your answer which is backed up with well selected evidence. You must be explicit in your answer, i.e. refer to the concept of 'success' throughout.

You should clarify your key points before you start. Below are some examples for you to consider.

- The United States was only partially successful in supporting the free who were resisting subjugation. This was because events in eastern Europe were beyond the control of the Americans after Potsdam.
- However the Americans were successful in containing communism as suggested by the Truman Doctrine.

### Questions in the style of OCR (Unit 3)

**Q** 2a **Explain how much of a threat to world peace was the Cuban Missile Crisis.** (30)

### How to answer this question

The question is asking you to show your understanding of the significance of the crisis. To reach the top bands you will need to place the Crisis into the context of the international situation, the relationship between the USA and the Soviet Union and the roles played by Khrushchev and Kennedy.

Below is an extract from an answer to this question. Note how the candidate has attempted to answer the question directly.

The Cuban Missile Crisis proved a considerable threat to world peace. This is because it became the focal point of the Cold War. It also was the situation in which the determination of the United States to resist the spread of communism came face to face with Soviet determination to protect the spread of communism.

The Crisis was also the climax of an arms race that had developed throughout the 1950s and 60s. It was the climax of growing tension which had seen the U2 crisis, Bay of Pigs fiasco and the building of the Berlin Wall. Therefore the threat to peace as the Crisis unfolded should not be underestimated.

**Q 2b Compare the importance of at least three reasons why North Vietnam won the Vietnam War.** (60)

### How to answer this question

You should try and make sure that you prioritise the reasons you have chosen and compare them in terms of relative importance. Therefore an argument should be planned before you start with a paragraph-by-paragraph structure.

Here are examples of the type of points you could choose to make:
- the Vietcong fought an effective guerilla campaign that served to destroy American morale at the front and at home
- the North Vietnamese had vitally important military backing from the Soviet Union and China
- the coverage of the Vietnam campaign in the world's press and the length of time the war lasted fuelled anti-war demonstrations that increased the unpopularity of the war in the United States.

### Further questions in the style of AQA (Unit 1)

Read Source A and then answer the questions.

**Source A** Adapted from a speech by US President Eisenhower at the 1959 summit with Khrushchev.

There must be some way to develop some kind of free city which might somehow be part of West Germany.....the time is coming, and perhaps soon, when we would simply have to get our forces out.

Q 1a Explain what Eisenhower proposed by 'free city' in the context of Berlin's status post war. (3)

  b Explain why Eisenhower made this speech at this time. (7)

  c How and why did American policy towards Berlin change in the period 1949–62? (15)

# Chapter 7
# The USA, 1919–68

## Section 1: The boom years and the Depression

### The 'Red Scare'

The First World War led to widespread patriotism and dislike of foreigners. This was encouraged by the Espionage Act of 1917 and the Sedition Act of 1918. Such intolerance was further fuelled by the Russian Revolution and the increased fear of the spread of communism. In 1919, when President Wilson was unwell, a 'Red Scare' was encouraged by the Attorney General **Mitchell Palmer**. Earlier in the year Palmer had been the victim of an unsuccessful assassination plot. This was the trigger for a nationwide attack on foreigners and anyone suspected of communist sympathies, such as the groups known as the Industrial Workers of the World. Five members of the New York Assembly were sacked for being socialists. On 1 January 1920 over 6,000 aliens were arrested and deported in what became known as the **Palmer Raids**. Such intolerance shocked many Americans including the new president Warren G. Harding who was elected in 1920. However even Harding agreed with the calls for greater restrictions on immigration which came from groups such as the National Security League. In May 1921 the Immigration Act set a quota on immigrants from any one country to 3% of persons of that country born and living in the USA, as counted by the 1910 census. This was followed by the **National Origins Act** of 1924 which put a ceiling on total immigration of 164,000 a year.

### Vanzetti and Sacco

At the height of the Red Scare two Italians were arrested and charged with the murder of a postmaster in Massachusetts. **Bartolomeo Vanzetti** and **Nicola Sacco** were immigrant anarchists, who had avoided military service. The evidence against them was far from conclusive. Their cause became celebrated throughout the world. Despite an appeal and the appointment of a committee to look into the men's trial they were executed in 1927.

### The Ku Klux Klan

Refounded in 1915, this group attacked African-Americans, Catholics and Jews. In the mid-1920s it seemed that the Klan was growing in strength to become a national organisation. It had a membership of around 5 million and practised torture and intimidation in many states across America. However, the Klan's popularity had peaked by 1926. A series of sexual and corruption scandals such as the conviction of Indiana Klan leader **David Stephenson** destroyed the image presented by the organisation.

## African-Americans

Many African-Americans did not benefit from the boom of the 1920s. Economic exclusion was compounded by political discrimination encouraged by the atmosphere of intolerance. Most African-Americans were prevented from voting in primary elections.

- As a result of poverty and the actions of the Klan many African-Americans moved to the cities in the industrial north. Initially this migration sparked off race riots such as that in Chicago in 1919 in which 38 people were killed.
- In many cites racial segregation was maintained with African-Americans inhabiting over-crowded slums. In 1925 **Harlem** in New York had a population density of 1,334 per hectare.
- However there was an increase in black consciousness as a result of the migration into the cities. The **Universal Negro Improvement Association** was founded by **Marcus Garvey** and by 1921 it had one million members. Harlem became the centre of a black cultural flowering led by the writer **Weldon Johnson**.

## Prohibition

In December 1917 Congress submitted to the States of America the **18th Amendment** to the constitution which banned the sale or manufacture of alcohol. The amendment was formalised in October 1919 by the **Volstead Act**. Organisations such as the **Anti-Saloon League** of America had been promoting the temperance cause (prohibition) across the United States for 50 years. Prohibition brought quick fortunes to those who broke the law. Bootleggers ran speakeasies (illegal bars) where illicit alcohol was drunk. Organised crime flourished and continued to do so after the disastrous social experiment had been abandoned in December 1933.

## The economic boom in the 1920s

The boom of the 1920s was built on the growth in consumer industries and the widely available credit facilities. The war had stimulated improvements in technology, methods of production and management techniques. After the war these improvements led to the reduction in the cost of consumer goods to the extent that they became available to a mass market.

- By 1927 the **Ford Motor Company** had sold 15 million **Model T** cars. The success of Ford was due to the efficient techniques of conveyor belt mass production and a highly skilled and well paid workforce.
- **General Motors** and **Buick** followed Ford's example and by 1929 America was producing over 6 million cars a year and car ownership in the United States totalled around 26 million.

- Other industries boomed, for example the expenditure on radios increased from $10 million in 1920 to $411 million in 1929.

## Farmers and textiles

The benefits of the boom of the 1920s were not universally enjoyed. The agricultural sector of the economy suffered from the consequences of overproduction, low prices and protectionism.
- Low prices in particular had a crippling effect, for example the bushel price of wheat fell from $1.82 in 1920 to 38 cents in 1932.
- A policy of protectionism failed to help. In May 1921 an **Emergency Tariff Act** raised duties on agricultural produce thereby reducing the volume of foreign trade.
- By 1924 some 600,000 families had lost their farms. The farm population was one and a half million people lower in 1930 than it had been in 1920.
- Despite the obvious plight of many in rural America, the laissez-faire attitude of successive administrations prevented significant government intervention.
- Legislation designed to help farmers, the **McNary–Haugen Bill**, was defeated in the House of Representatives in 1924 and 1926. When it was finally passed it was vetoed by President Coolidge in 1927. It was not until June 1929 and the **Agricultural Administration Act** that the Hoover administration enacted its rescue plan for farmers.
- The cotton industry also remained depressed throughout the 1930s. In 1921 30% of the cotton crop was destroyed by the boll weevil. The New England textile industry suffered from increasing competition from the south and 90,000 jobs were lost between 1922–33.

## Weaknesses in the economy

Wages rose throughout the 1920s. However the economic structure was not secure.
- In 1922 the **Ford-McCumber Tariff Act** was passed which imposed high tariffs on imported goods. The result was that whilst American industry was protected, there was little scope for foreign trade.
- These tarriffs also meant that the benefits (low retail prices) of the new mass production techniques were not fully passed on to the consumer.
- As has been pointed out, not all of American society shared in the boom of the 1920s, a factor which also limited demand. Only 5% of the population had 33% of the income.
- Too many goods were bought on credit. The amount of credit grew from $45.3 billion in 1921 to $73 billion in 1929.
- By 1928 the economy began to slow. The new **Model A** car produced by Ford failed to sell at expected levels. However instead of lowering prices, Ford and other businesses laid off workers.

- Around the same time in 1928 a speculation frenzy gripped the stock market. However the market was vastly over-inflated in value and much speculation was based on credit. The speculation was unrestrained with the numbers of investors reaching around a quarter of the American population.

## Crash

The economic downturn in the key industries of car manufacture and building sparked a cash crisis which led to the **Wall Street Crash**.
- 'Black Tuesday', 29 October 1929, saw investors beginning to sell all stocks and shares in an attempt to recoup some of their investment.
- The collapse in confidence which followed led to a collapse in confidence in the whole financial system.
- The network of small independent banks across America was vulnerable to this collapse in confidence. By 1932 over 5000 banks had folded with around 9 million investors losing their savings.
- The depression was worsened by the international collapse in confidence.
- This was not helped by the **Smoot-Hawley Tariff Act** signed in July 1930 which raised tariffs further on imported goods. By the end of 1931 some 25 countries had retaliated by imposing tariffs on imported American goods.
- **Unemployment** rose from 3.2% in 1929 to 24.9% in 1933 and as many as 13 million Americans were without an income. The collapse in demand had a devastating impact on agriculture with farm income falling by two-thirds between 1929–1932.

## Roosevelt's election

By late 1932 the banking system was close to complete collapse. In Washington a large group of First World War veterans, known as the '**Bonus Army**', petitioned President Hoover for their war bonus, but they were dismissed by the army. In the November Presidential election, the Democrat candidate **Franklin D. Roosevelt** campaigned against Hoover's brand of '**rugged individualism**'. Roosevelt promised government intervention and a '**New Deal**' for Americans. He had a spectacular victory, winning 472 electoral votes to Hoover's 59. On taking office Roosevelt acted quickly to restore confidence in the financial system.

## The First Hundred Days

Roosevelt embarked on a frenzy of legislation to deal with the crisis.
- The banks were closed for four days and only reopened after the passage of the **Emergency Banking Act** (March 1933).
- His administration acted quickly to shore up the collapsing agricultural economy with a spate of legislation including the **Agricultural**

**Adjustment Act** (May 1933) and the **Farm Credit Act** (June 1933).
- The unemployed were drafted into work through the creation of the **Civilian Conservation Corps** (March 1933) and aid given through the federal **Emergency Relief Act** (May 1933).
- Further legislation was passed on mortgages, securities, labour relations and the **Tennessee Valley Authority** was created to provide electricity to the region.

## The First New Deal

The First Hundred Days went some way to restoring confidence. However Roosevelt's initiatives needed to be financed and the prospect of higher taxation offended many important sections of American society. Roosevelt also failed to deal with the issue of protectionism. In 1933 his delegate at the London Conference was recalled rather than back plans to improve world trade. Although the **Trade Agreements Act** was passed in 1934 protectionism remained.
- Roosevelt attempted to restore American prosperity through the **Alphabet Agencies**. The most prominent of these, the **National Recovery Administration** (NRA) was created by the **National Industrial Recovery Act** (NIRA). Its original powers were to regulate and enforce codes of conduct for American industry.
- Such was the opposition to the NRA that in 1935 the **Supreme Court** declared it unconstitutional and showed the limitations of the New Deal to carry out change.
- The **Public Works Administration** however, transformed the American landscape and gave work to millions.
- The **Agricultural Adjustment Administration** rescued agriculture despite the dust storms of 1934 and 1935 which ravaged the mid-west.

## The Second New Deal

Despite an improvement in confidence, the New Deal failed to resolve the problem of America's industrial sector.
- Unemployment was reduced but still remained stubbornly high; by 1937 it had fallen to 7.7. million but rose again in 1938 to 10.4 million.
- There was criticism of Roosevelt's policies from the left, spearheaded by **Senator Huey Long**, and from the right. However, he won the 1936 presidential election by a landslide.

The Second New Deal, beginning from 1935, was aimed at improving the welfare of Americans.
- The **Social Security Act** was passed in 1935 to help the elderly and unemployed. To pay for improved welfare provision the **Wealth–Tax Act**, which increased taxes on the wealthy, was passed to pay for the increased

welfare provision. In October 1938 the **Wages and Hours Law** prohibited child labour.

- However, Roosevelt continued to meet with fierce opposition in the Supreme Court. In 1936 the court blocked many New Deal measures which brought to a head a constitutional crisis. In 1938 Roosevelt attacked the Supreme Court by attempting to retire any judges over 70. However Congress refused to back him in his battle and he was defeated.
- Roosevelt also had to face a rash of labour disputes in 1937 in the steel and car industries. The **Wagner Act** (which the Supreme Court also tried to block) was passed with the aim of regulating the unionisation of many industries.

Despite the fact that critics of the New Deal claimed that it had run out of steam by the late 1930s Roosevelt's role in saving American democracy should not be underestimated.

# Assessment: The boom years and the Depression

## Questions in the style of Edexcel (Unit 1)

Read the sources carefully and then answer the questions which follow.

**Source A** A record of the enforcement of Prohibition, 1920. From *The Dry Decade* by Merz Charles.

> January 16: The law took effect.
>
> March 10: Federal agents in Brooklyn began a round up of druggists (chemists) accused of selling whisky without a prescription from a doctor.
>
> May 24: Dr Charles W. Eliot of Harvard University declared in an address at Boston that people with money and position were helping to defeat the law.
>
> June 6: The special train of the Massachusetts delegation to the Republican National Convention was raided by prohibition agents who seized its stock of liquor.
>
> July 2: Jail sentences aggregating 59 months and fines totalling $85,000 were imposed on officials of two companies in New York City, found guilty of withdrawing 25,000 gallons of industrial alcohol which were diverted to beverage purposes.

**Source B** Adapted from a letter written by John D. Rockefeller in 1932. The Rockefellers were wealthy industrialists.

> I hoped that prohibition would be supported by the public and thus the day hastened when the value to society of men with minds and bodies free from the undermining effects of alcohol would be generally realised. That this has not been the result, but rather that drinking has generally increased; that the speakeasy has replaced the saloon...that a vast army of lawbreakers has been recruited and financed on a colossal scale...that respect for the law has been greatly lessened; that crime has increased to an unprecedented degree I have slowly and reluctantly come to believe.

**Source C** The notorious gangster Al Capone speaking in 1927.

What's Al Capone done, then? He has supplied a legitimate demand. Some call it bootlegging. Some call it racketeering. I call it business. They say I violate the prohibition law. Who doesn't?

**Source D** Arrests and seizures made by Federal Prohibition agents. From *Modern America* by John Vick, 1985.

|  | 1921 | 1925 | 1929 |
|---|---|---|---|
| Illegal distilleries seized | 9,746 | 12,023 | 15,794 |
| Gallons of distilled spirits seized | 414,000 | 1,103,000 | 1,186,000 |
| Numbers of persons aarrested | 34,175 | 62,747 | 66,878 |

**Source E** Adapted from *Organised Crime in Chicago* by John Landesco.

The Capone Gang is an organisation of professional gangsters... The gang was formed for the business administration of establishments of vice, gambling and booze. Although many of these establishments are reported as owned by Capone, closer examination shows that they have separate owners but are under the political and physical protection of Capone and his gang.

Q   1a  **Study Sources A and D. What does the sources tell you about the difficulties faced by the police in enforcing prohibition?**        **(3)**

## How to answer this question

To answer this question you should try to do the following:
*   sum up in your own words what the source reveals about the enforcement of prohibition
*   quote briefly from the source.

**Style** Here is an extract from an answer to this question. Note how the candidate infers from the sources and then uses one of them for evidence.

**Q   b Study Source B. Using your own knowledge explain why prohibition failed.** (4)

## How to answer this question

The key to answering this question is the organisation of your information and clear planning.

**Plan** You need to ensure that your answer focuses on reasons why prohibition failed. Before you start you should write in your plan the key themes. Here are some examples.
- Prohibition failed because significant social groups ignored the legislation and flouted the law.
- Prohibition failed because of the efforts of organised crime to provide alcohol.

**Q   c Study Sources C and E. How far does Source C support the interpretation of Source E in explaining the activities of Al Capone?** (5)

## How to answer this question

In order to write a well rewarded response to this question you need to ensure that you include information from both sources. Further advice on how to compare sources can be found in Chapter 2 on page 12.

**Style** Here is an extract from a good quality response which attempts to answer the question.

**Q    d** Study Sources B and C. How useful are these two sources as evidence of the problems of enforcing the prohibition laws? **(5)**

## How to answer this question

You need to make sure that you do the following when answering this question:
- briefly plan your answer taking into account the positive points and limitations of the sources
- you will need to refer to, and select information from, the sources.

Further advice on how to answer questions on the utility of sources can be found on page 11 of Chapter 2.

**Style** You should try and explain each point you make, quote where necessary and cover as many points as possible. Below is an extract from an answer to this question. The candidate has attempted to deal with this question in this style.

> The main limitation to Source B is that it is a very subjective viewpoint. Rockefeller is writing from an idealistic viewpoint and puts the issue of prohibition very much into the context of his hope that it would alter American society. The Source is extremely useful, however, in showing that prohibition was the product of such idealistic aims, e.g. Rockefeller writes of his hopes of when the 'value to society of men with minds and bodies free from the undermining effects of alcohol would be generally realised'. However, as Capone's evidence shows, such idealism was bound to lose out to the hard-headed realism of 'business'.

**Q    e** Use your own knowledge and the information from Sources A and E. How far do you agree with the view that Prohibition was a social disaster? **(12)**

## How to answer this question

You are asked to give an analytical answer to this question. The main focus of your answer must be on the impact of Prohibition. To be awarded the top marks you need to do the following:
- argue using the sources and your own knowledge
- link overproduction with other factors, in particular the nature of demand and protectionism
- show that you can sustain a judgement throughout the question.

**Style** Below is an extract to an answer to this question. The candidate has sustained an argument in a direct style throughout the answer.

Perhaps the most significant impact of Prohibition was the effect it had on respect for the law and the development of organised crime. It was not just the rise in influence of gangsters such as Al Capone as shown in Source E but the extent of that influence. More significant was that the law was flouted by those in authority. From the start in 1920, the law enforcement agencies had to battle against widespread undermining of the law. In doing so, many of the law enforcement officers became corrupt and willing to accept bribes. It is difficult to underestimate the impact of this undermining of the law.

## Course essay question in the style of AQA

Q **2 Why did the American economy collapse into depression from 1929?**

## How to answer this question

To achieve high marks you need to think about the following:
- the key to a successful course essay is a long and detailed plan
- your main points of argument need to be clearly thought through
- you need to link the main factors together in your plan and throughout your essay.

**Plan** Below are examples of the points you might put at the start of the plan.
- the depression was the result of important structural weaknesses in the American economy, not least the nature of demand and the problem of overproduction.
- these weaknesses were compounded by the accumulation of debt through the extension of credit
- the Wall Street Crash was caused by a downturn in confidence. Its main consequences were to deepen the depression.

## Further questions in the style of AQA course essays

Q **3 What was the impact of the Ku Klux Klan on American society in the 1920s?**

Q **4 How successfully did the First New Deal solve America's economic problems?**

# Section 2: War and civil rights, 1939–68

## 1939–41

It was the outbreak of war in Europe which was to signal a return to full employment in the United States. In 1939 America remained overwhelmingly isolationist, the **Neutrality Act** of 1936 stressing strict neutrality. However Roosevelt ordered preparations to strengthen America's defences which were to give a substantial boost to the economy.

- In January 1939 he asked Congress for $552 million to update defences.
- On 5 September 1939 America declared her neutrality in the war although the Neutrality Act was amended in November to allow the sale of American weapons.
- By 1941 Roosevelt finally believed it was in the United States' interest materially to support the British Empire which stood virtually alone against the Axis powers.
- The **Lend Lease Act** of March 1941 empowered the President to provide goods and services to countries 'whose defence the President deems vital to the defence of the United States'. By 1945, over $50.6 billion worth of aid had been granted.

## War

The mobilisation of resources which followed the Japanese attack on **Pearl Harbor** on 7 December and the German declaration of war on the United States on 11 December was to transform the American economy.

- In the first year of war the United States produced 24,000 tanks and 48,000 planes. The wartime boom outstripped that of the 1920s; between 1940–45 steel production rose by 20% and that of fuel oils by 44%.
- The wartime economy was organised through agencies which evolved out of the New Deal. Many of the old agencies worked side by side with the new bodies such as the **War Production Board**. An example was the **Reconstruction Finance Corporation** which assumed a new importance organising American industry and finance. In many senses the war economy was a natural successor to the New Deal. Many of those who had directed the New Deal such as Harry Hopkins or Henry J Kaiser turned their management and entrepreneurial skills to the business of winning the war.
- Productivity soared after the adoption of new techniques. In 1942 General Electric's marine turbine production increased by $299 million.
- Building also on the tradition of state research, Roosevelt created the **Office of Scientific Research and Development** in 1941 out of which evolved the **Manhattan Project**. Over the next three years the project perfected the application of atomic energy to the weapons of destruction at a cost of $2 billion.

## African-Americans in the 1940s and 1950s

The war presented African-Americans with job opportunities. However segregation was preserved in civilian life and in the military. Despite the opening of new factories across America, many of them initially refused to employ African-Americans. Under intense pressure from black leader **A Philip Randoph**, Roosevelt issued presidential **Executive Order 8802** which banned racial discrimination in the workplace. The **National Association for the Advancement of Coloured People** (NAACP) campaigned against discrimination. In 1944 it won a landmark Supreme Court case, *Smith v Allwright*, in which the white-only primary election was declared unconstitutional. Although there were still tensions, (in Detroit 34 people were killed in a race riot in 1943), advances were made, as for example when the Marine Corps opened its ranks to black servicemen and when in 1945 the first integrated unit was formed. The trend towards integration was highlighted by President Truman's decision to abolish the race quota for the armed services in 1948.

## Protest and Martin Luther King

In the 1950s NAACP took its challenge to white supremacy and the concept of segregation in schools into the courts.
- In 1954 the Supreme Court declared segregation unacceptable in the case of *Brown v Topeka Board of Education*.
- This decision was tested at **Little Rock High School** in 1957 where troops had to be sent to uphold the concept of desegregation.
- In December 1955 an African-American women **Rosa Parks** ignored a southern custom and refused to give up her seat on a bus to a white person. Parks was imprisoned but her incarceration sparked off a boycott of the buses. In 1956 the Supreme Court found that segregation on buses in Alabama was unlawful.

The campaign against segregation was led by Martin Luther King, a Baptist Minister who believed that change could be provoked through peaceful means. As **President of the Southern Christian Leadership Conference**, King became the leader of the peaceful campaign to achieve equal rights.
- In February 1960 a small group of African-American students asked to be served at the whites-only food counter at Woolworths in Greensboro, North Carolina. On refusal they began a 'sit- in' which became the main tactic of the protesters. It was used effectively by the '**Freedom Riders**' who challenged segregation on the nation's buses in 1961.

## Further protest

Despite the election of J F Kennedy as President in 1960, Federal government action in support of the civil rights movement was painfully slow. Kennedy set up a **Committee on Equal Employment Opportunity** to monitor for racial discrimination, but did little else. Progress therefore had to be won by the civil rights movement.

- In 1962 an African-American student, **James Meredith**, attempted to enrol as the first black student at the University of Mississippi. Supported by the NAACP and Dr King, Meredith was eventually enrolled but at the cost of 2 lives and 375 wounded in the ensuing riot by those determined to keep him out.
- In 1963 a series of huge demonstrations took place to support the case for civil rights. In **Birmingham, Alabama** King was jailed twice before local authorities agreed to desegregate the town. The demonstrations climaxed with a march on Washington in August 1963 which involved some 250,000 protesters. The Kennedy administration was sufficiently moved by the demonstration to promise civil rights legislation. Despite Kennedy's assassination in November 1963 this promise was honoured by the new president Lyndon Johnson.

## Civil Rights Act

In 1964 the Civil Rights Act gave the Federal government the power to ban racial discrimination. The process of dismantling segregation was to be handled by two new bodies, the **Community Relations Service** and the **Equal Employment Opportunity Commission**. However there had been considerable opposition to the Act, in particular from southern Democrats in the Senate. Therefore Lyndon Johnson made compromises in order to get the legislation through. One notable clause which was left out was one which insisted on racial quotas. However white opposition in the south to equal rights was clear.

- In the summer of 1964 the Ku Klux Klan inspired a spate of attacks on African-Americans.
- Many state governments showed a reluctance to register their votes. Lyndon Johnson's response was to threaten to send federal registrars to the south in order to register African-American voters. Many southern states feared federal interference and improved the procedure themselves.
- In 1965 250,000 new voters were registered.

## Violent protest

Conditions for African-Americans in northern cities were often bad, with poor education and slum housing marring the lives of many families. It was in this environment that organisations which rejected Martin Luther King's pacifism flourished.

- The Nation of Islam preached a message of separatism and violence. A leading figure in the movement was Malcolm X whose calls for violence placed considerable pressure on Martin Luther King.
- The 'Black Power' group led by **Stokely Carmichael** similarly urged a more direct approach. In 1963 there were rent strikes in Harlem, New

York and in 1965 the **Watts** district of Los Angeles erupted into violence which left 34 dead. Over the next three years there were around 150 riots in many cities including Chicago, Detroit and Atlanta.

- The cause of the riots was primarily economic but they were also a reflection of the slow pace of social change and the frustration that this caused. A clear example was when Martin Luther King attempted to persuade the Chicago city administration to end its housing segregation policy. The mayor, **Richard Daley**, was unwilling to cooperate and the hostility shown to King and his followers was such that they were forced to end their protest in Chicago.

## The extent to which civil rights had been achieved by 1968

In April 1968 Martin Luther King was assassinated. At the time of his death there was a considerable way to go in the struggle for civil rights. Whilst political equality had been achieved, the African-American population had not achieved social or economic equality. There were attempts to legislate to improve the conditions of America's urban population:

- In 1968 Lyndon Johnson's administration promoted the **Open Housing Act** which attempted to end racial discrimination in housing.
- However discrimination in this and other areas continued. The federal government under Lyndon Johnson was, as it had been under Kennedy, reluctant to tackle the fundamental issues.
- Poverty persisted with around a third of the African-American families living below the poverty line. The Vietnam War diverted resources which might otherwise have been used for social improvement. The 'second reconstruction' of the 1960s had only partly improved the condition of African-American's in the US.

How to Pass AS Modern World History